W9-AKD-339

PASTORAL CARE OF ALCOHOL ABUSERS

Creative Pastoral Care and Counseling Series
Howard W. Stone, Editor

Books in the Series

CREATIVE PASTORAL CARE AND COUNSELING SERIES

PASTORAL CARE OF ALCOHOL ABUSERS

Andrew J. Weaver and Harold G. Koenig

FORTRESS PRESS   MINNEAPOLIS

PASTORAL CARE FOR ALCOHOL ABUSERS

Cover design: Paul Boehnke

Library of Congress Cataloging-in-Publication Data

Koenig, Harold G. (Harold George), 1951-
  Pastoral care of alcohol abusers / Harold G. Koenig and Andrew J. Weaver.
    p. cm. — (Creative pastoral care and counseling series)
  Includes bibliographical references.
  ISBN 978-0-8006-6261-5 (alk. paper)
  1. Church work with alcoholics. 2. Pastoral counseling. I. Weaver, Andrew J., 1947- II. Title.
  BV4460.5.K64 2009
  259'.4292--dc22
                                        2009025328

Manufactured in the U.S.A.

"To my best friend, something I didn't realize until it was too late"

CONTENTS

EDITOR'S FOREWORD

I don't think I had served in congregational ministry for more than two weeks when the wife of an alcohol abuser knocked on my door. She was at her wits' end. Her husband was a weekend binge drinker whose behavior was damaging their marriage and their family life. She wanted to know what to do about his drinking but also worried about the effect on their eleven-year-old twin boys. Her story, and similar stories of many others since then, helped me to realize how important it is to have a plan for offering care to individuals and families troubled by the effects of alcohol.

Pastoral Care of Alcohol Abusers is written for clergy and those who work in the church as a resource when they care for individuals (and their loved ones) who suffer from alcohol addiction and its related problems, such as depression, psychological trauma, gambling, or grief. A genius of this book is the depth and variety of its authors' experience and information—Andrew Weaver was a minister and a psychologist, and Harold Koenig is a physician (psychiatrist) who has done extensive research on the nexus between religion and health. The resulting breadth and depth of the book makes it a resource that clergy can rely upon in a wide array of situations that they encounter in their ministry.

Five case studies form the core of *Pastoral Care of Alcohol Abusers*. As readers enter the lives of the individuals who people these cases, they gain helpful information on how to understand and care for alcohol abusers. Take, for example, the depressed sixteen-year-old girl we meet in the first case. In the background for the case, Weaver and Koenig quote a statistic that astounded me: by the time an average teenager is eighteen, he or she has seen up to one hundred thousand television beer commercials. In this case, the authors share ways in which clergy, the church, and mental health workers can offer effective care for the teen and her family. They also suggest further writings that allow readers to go into more depth if they wish to explore issues raised by this case.

Pastoral Care of Alcohol Abusers includes an important discussion of the usefulness of twelve-step programs such as

Alcoholics Anonymous (AA). Groups like AA, frequently meeting in churches, have long been the backbone of the church's care for families affected by drinking problems. The book suggests a number of additional organizations that are useful for families troubled by alcohol abuse—as well as for clergy and others who offer them care.

Much of the care for families experiencing alcohol abuse occurs in the church community, and the authors discuss important supports and interventions within the congregation's ministry. Sometimes a case calls for referral to an outside therapist or agency, however. It has been my experience that referring someone within your care is not an easy task, especially when alcohol is involved. Weaver and Koenig provide a number of useful strategies for making outside referrals that stick.

Throughout the centuries, the church's theological response to the use and abuse of alcohol and drugs has varied. Sometimes the problem drinker was cast out of the church (and even the community), incarcerated, or even worse; at other times the church has looked the other way, unwilling to address the problem. Today, enlightened ministers and other church leaders offering care to the alcohol addicted can benefit from several metaphors of ministry found in Scripture. At times the pastoral caregiver operates from a prophetic stance, calling troubled persons to own up to their behavior and make the changes necessary to address them. At other times the classic shepherding stance is appropriate, assisting families to find the help they need to combat the impact of alcohol abuse. In still other cases, pastoral caregivers function as wounded healers, not as individuals who are in some way superior but as fellow sufferers; a theology of the cross influences how they care for others. *Pastoral Care of Alcohol Abusers* draws on all three of these theological metaphors as they craft a response to families affected by the abuse of alcohol or drugs.

One topic I personally found most useful in *Pastoral Care of Alcohol Abusers* is the discussion of related problems such as depression, gambling, various family issues, and grief. Another uniquely helpful chapter examines the problem of the retired drinker. I first encountered this problem when I worked in a pastoral counseling agency in Arizona. Many people who have retired fill in their free time with drinking, resulting in tremendous disruption in their lives and their marriages. Weaver and Koenig offer a very useful design for addressing alcohol abuse in retirement, and I wish I had read this chapter in my Arizona days.

I am confident that *Pastoral Care of Alcohol Abusers* will enhance your understanding of alcohol abuse and enrich your ministry to individuals and families who are struggling with this threat. Weaver and Koenig bring to their work the wisdom of many combined years of experience, both in research and in care for individuals and families troubled by alcohol abuse; the scope and quality of the care you offer to others is certain to benefit from their knowledge and sound guidance.

Howard W. Stone

IN MEMORIAM

This book was in its final stages of writing and editing when Andrew Weaver died very suddenly on October 22, 2008. Andrew was only sixty-one years old. He was a United Methodist minister and psychologist, married to another minister, Dr. Carolyn L. Stapleton. He possessed a prodigious talent, was a superb and highly productive researcher in the field of religion and health and a compassionate pastoral caregiver. He was my friend.

Andrew was not a shy person.

I remember our first contact. He called me, out of the blue, wanting to chat. He said we had work in common. That first conversation led to many phone calls, jazz at the Village Vanguard in New York City, the publishing of one book, the editing of two other books, and a series of articles that we coauthored. The calls kept coming.

A friendship grew. Whenever Andrew called, I found a comfortable chair because this was not going to be a five-minute business call; it would be a long, wide-ranging conversation that might cover some business at hand, but inevitably would veer to politics, publishing, our latest research ventures, jazz, theater, art, and life. Besides being one of the most accomplished researchers in the area of religion and mental health, Andrew was a keen and thoughtful observer of life on this planet as we live it today. I always learned from his observations on the church, politics, social change, or relationships.

Whenever I had a research question, he was the one I called. Now Andrew is gone. I will miss those conversations and his friendship. I will miss his intelligence, creativity, and psychic energy. I will miss collaborating with him. I will miss his passion for the church, for the arts, for life.

And I will miss his out-of-the-blue telephone calls.

Howard W. Stone

ACKNOWLEDGMENTS

Dr. Harold G. Koenig, Dr. Howard W. Stone, and the staff of Fortress Press gratefully acknowledge the Reverend Carolyn Stapleton for her invaluable editorial assistance in the completion of this final volume by her late husband, the Rev. Dr. Andrew C. Weaver.

Introduction

ALCOHOL, CLERGY, AND FAITH

With 120 million American teens and adults using alcohol, its abuse is a significant public health issue across the life span (SAMHSA, 2003). Young people between the ages of eighteen and twenty-four spend billions of dollars annually on beer alone. By the time the average teen is eighteen years old, he or she has been exposed to one hundred thousand television beer commercials (Parrott, 1993). A Harvard University survey found that more than eight in ten administrators of four-year colleges viewed students' alcohol use as a problem on campus (Wechsler et al., 2004).

A recent study by the Centers for Disease Control and Prevention found 45 percent of teens reported they had consumed alcohol in the past month and 64 percent of those who imbibed said they were binge drinking, defined as having five or more alcoholic drinks in a row (Miller et al., 2007). Each year approximately five thousand persons under the age of twenty-one die from alcohol-related car accidents, injuries, homicides, and suicides (National Institute on Alcohol Abuse and Alcoholism, 2005). The annual economic costs of alcohol abuse in the United States have been estimated at $184.6 billion (Harwood, 2000).

Given the magnitude of the problem, it is important that clergy be skilled in recognizing alcoholism and its related issues (Hatchett et al., 2007). Research over several decades has demonstrated that millions of Americans call upon clergy for help in times of trouble, including dealing with problems related to addiction (Weaver, 1995). The 353,000 clergy serving congregations in the United States are among the most trusted professionals in society (Gallup and Lindsay, 1999).

Pastors are often in long-term relationships with individuals and their families, which enables them to observe changes in behavior that may indicate early signs of alcoholism and related problems. Furthermore, clergy are accessible helpers within communities that have established patterns of responding to crises. Pastors can help persons with alcohol difficulties connect with mental health professionals.

There is a clear need to train clergy in the area of alcohol abuse (Hatchett et al., 2007). Researchers asked rabbis and Protestant ministers in California to name training areas in which they could use the most help. The rabbis and ministers identified training in alcohol/drug problems as either the most important or second most important area for additional training (Ingram and Lowe, 1989; Lowe, 1986). In a survey of European-American and African-American clergy in Tennessee, researchers asked clergy about their level of confidence as a counselor. Drug and alcohol problems ranked next to last among the areas where the clergy felt confident to offer counsel (Mannon and Crawford, 1996).

The University of Texas Medical Center in Galveston surveyed 75 percent of the pastors in its community (Turner, 1995). It found no ongoing program in congregations for addicted persons, while a majority of the clergy expressed interest in learning more about addictions and enhancing their skills as counselors. Pastors also indicate that teen alcohol and drug use is a great concern. In a national survey of clergy, 55 percent indicated that alcohol and drug use was the greatest teen pastoral care concern in their congregation. In the same survey, only one in four of the pastors felt their church's ministry to teens with alcohol or drug problems was good (Rowatt, 1989).

At the same time, research findings consistently support the conclusion that public and private religious involvement can act as protective factors that decrease the potential that a young person will use alcohol and/or other drugs (Wills et al., 2003). Faith communities offer supportive environments that can reinforce family attitudes and teachings against alcohol abuse. Increased family and teen religious involvement has been linked to lower levels of substance abuse and negative attitudes toward substance use. One study in the United States examined a sample of 13,250 students in grades seven to twelve (Bahr et al., 1993). The researchers found that the greater the religious involvement, the less likely it is that a teen will use alcohol, marijuana, amphetamines, or depressants. Adolescents who are involved in faith-based activities are also less likely to have friends who use alcohol and illicit drugs.

This book will address a number of issues of concern to clergy and to those who come to them for guidance about alcohol and such related difficulties as depression, psychological trauma, and gambling. Given the size of the problem, one can assume that there will be a continued need for clergy and other religious profession-als to offer informed help. It is important for them to learn how to recognize alcoholism competently, identify when to make refer-rals, help persons find available community resources, and train members of their congregations to provide support to affected individuals and families (Hatchett et al., 2007).

HOW TO USE THE BOOK

Pastoral Care of Alcohol Abusers is designed as a basic text for all those who are in ministry, as well as a resource for those train-ing for pastoral ministry. It is written for people of all faiths, with an appreciation for the richness of the intergenerational and mul-ticultural diversity found in religious communities. Its primary audience is clergy and other pastoral workers who work with indi-viduals experiencing alcohol and related problems, such as depres-sion, psychological trauma, gambling, or grief reactions. The book takes a practical approach based on current research. The reader is able to quickly and easily locate information about a range of alcohol abuse and related issues.

Included in each clinical case is information about how a pastor can assess the problem, what aspects of the case are most important, how to identify the major issues, specific directions about what a pastor and congregation can do, when to refer to a mental health specialists, and information about resources that can provide help. National organizations (often with toll-free numbers and Internet addresses) that supply information and sup-port for families facing these issues are identified for each concern addressed. Sections on the value of twelve-step programs and how to make an effective referral as well as a glossary of technical terms are found in the last part of the book.

1

CASE STUDY #1:
THE DEPRESSED TEEN

"She was moody and withdrawn."

Reverend Lisa Dunn is pastor of a medium-sized church in the Midwest, in which the Jordan family has been involved for several years. They became especially active after the death of their youngest son from leukemia one year ago. Their sixteen-year-old daughter, Jean, had become noticeably withdrawn from both family and friends in the past several months and had become less interested in her appearance. Jean stopped participating in the youth group and her grades dropped at school. She was moody and had become pessimistic in her outlook toward life. She developed a short fuse and complained of feeling worthless. Recently, friends reported that they had seen Jean drinking with a group of older students after school. Jean had been very close to her younger brother and appeared to have been the most affected by and least accepting of his death.

It is important to have an accurate picture of Jean's alcohol use and emotional state. The rapid and negative changes in her life suggest something serious has developed. Is she using alcohol in an attempt to cope with unresolved grief related to the death of her brother? It is not uncommon for alcohol and drug abuse to mask depression and grief reactions. Depression is one of the most common forms of emotional problems in young people. Experts estimate that about one in twenty teens is depressed (Reynolds, 1995), while one in four depressed adolescents use drugs or alcohol to cope with the problem (Fleming and Offord, 1990). The drop in Jean's grades may signal decreased concentration and slowed thinking, also common in depression.

The use of alcohol for self-medication is often the pattern of individuals with poor coping skills and high addictive potential. How much is Jean in denial about her alcohol abuse? Does she minimize her alcohol use? How much insight does Jean have into her problem?

RESPONSE TO VIGNETTE

Jean has many of the signs of a teen who has an alcohol abuse problem and depression: she has withdrawn from family and friends and has stopped activities she used to enjoy at church. She has difficulties at school and has had a significant negative change in her mood and thinking. Her family reports that Jean has decreased interest in her physical appearance. She may have developed peer relationships with youth who are using alcohol.

Reverend Dunn and Jean's parents decided to talk to Jean about her new behaviors. The pastor used her active listening skills while assessing Jean's emotional state. Reverend Dunn established a safe and caring relationship as she empathetically responded to Jean at the family home. The teen confessed increasing use of alcohol. When the pastor reminded Jean of how much her family loved her and was concerned about her, she broke down and wept. She began to express her deep grief over the death of her beloved brother. With gentleness and support, Reverend Dunn encouraged Jean to grieve her loss, understanding that each individual has a unique way to grieve, and that Jean will need to mourn her brother's death according to her inner timetable.

After Reverend Dunn and Jean's family had their intervention with her, Jean agreed to see a psychiatrist, Dr. Barbara Miller, who specializes in teenage substance abuse problems. The physician advised a medical examination to rule out physical problems that could have triggered the depression, but no underlying medical issue was found that would account for the depression. Jean was also assessed for antidepressant medications and was given a prescription to help her through the first several months.

Over months of therapy, it became clear that Jean had begun to rely on alcohol and was drinking to self-medicate her depression. Jean was successfully treated as an outpatient for alcohol abuse and depression.

The psychiatrist also noted that Jean's family needed to address its poor communication, which became pronounced after the death of her brother. Jean's substance abuse was, in part, a symptom of their pain as a family and their inability to express their anguish in a way that could bring healing. With several months of therapy, the family was able to develop deeper bonding and a renewed faith as they worked together through the crisis.

DIAGNOSTIC CRITERIA

Alcohol abuse involves a pattern of use characterized by negative, recurrent, and significant consequences. This diagnosis requires only one of the following criteria over the course of twelve months (APA, 2000):

1. Recurrent alcohol use results in a failure to fulfill major obligations at home or work (such as repeated neglect of school responsibilities).
2. Repeated use of alcohol in situations in which such use is known to be physically hazardous.
3. Recurrent alcohol related legal problems.
4. Continued use despite having persistent or recurrent social or interpersonal problems resulting from the effects of the alcohol (such as arguments with friends or family members about the consequences of using the substance).

An adolescent is diagnosed with a *major depression* when there have been two weeks or more of feeling sad, gloomy, depressed, irritable, or experiencing a loss of interest, motivation, or enjoyment in usual activities (APA, 2000). Along with a depressed mood or loss of interest, the person must also have had two or more weeks of at least four of the following eight symptoms:

- fatigue or loss of energy
- lethargy or increased restlessness (agitation)
- loss of appetite and weight or excessive appetite and weight gain
- difficulty sleeping or sleeping too much
- loss of social or sexual interest
- feelings of worthlessness or excessive guilt
- difficulty concentrating
- feeling that life is not worth living, wanting to die, or feeling suicidal

TREATMENT WITHIN THE FAITH COMMUNITY

Research has shown that stable families lower the risk of alcohol and drug abuse, so church programs that focus on strengthening the family can be a preventive strategy (Johnson et al., 1996). A strong youth program that promotes good communication and social skills is a valuable preventive measure as well. Teen alcohol and drug abusers tend to have poor assertion skills, high social anxiety, and low self-worth. Social skills training can enhance coping, self-control, social problem solving, negotiation skills, and assertiveness, as well as increasing the ability to resist peer pressure (Haggerty et al., 1989).

Encouraging teens and their families to be active in the life of the community of faith is itself an important preventive strategy when addressing substance abuse. Youth who practice their religious faith have more positive social values and caring behaviors and their families are more stable than those who do not practice their faith. Surveys have found that adolescent regular church attenders are half as likely to use alcohol as teens who do not attend church regularly (Gallup and Bezilla, 1992). These findings add to the extensive research supporting the social benefit of nurturing, nonpunitive religious practice in limiting and preventing alcohol and drug use (Gorsuch, 1995).

Religion can protect children and their parents against depression by acting as a buffer against stressful events. According to researchers at Columbia University, children whose mothers are religiously committed are less likely to suffer depression (Miller et al., 1997). The study found that the daughters of mothers for whom religion was highly important were 60 percent less likely to have a major depression. A second study found that frequent church attenders in Texas with high spiritual support had lower levels of depression than their peers without religious involvement (Wright et al., 1993).

Although many clergy report that depression is the most common problem that they are asked to help people overcome, they are often inadequately trained to identify depression or suicide risk (Weaver, 1995). In a national survey of clergy and pastoral care specialists, only one in four believed the church was offering helpful programs for depressed teenagers, and pastors ranked their effectiveness with teen depression as generally poor (Rowatt, 1989). The study underscores the need for clergy and other religious leaders to learn to recognize mental health problems in teenagers competently and to train members of their faith communities to provide emotional support to youth and their families. Positive social relationships outside one's immediate family are a protective factor against developing emotional problems like depression in at-risk youth (Huntley and Phelps, 1990).

TREATMENT BY MENTAL HEALTH SPECIALISTS

When considering referring a teen to a mental health professional, it is important to ask what plan of action the specialist will use. A pastor or other religious professional needs a basic understanding of standard treatment protocols to assess whether a mental health professional is knowledgeable and experienced in treating teens and their families. Here is an example of the sort of treatment considerations one would make in a treatment plan for an adolescent suffering from alcohol abuse.

In the beginning, a therapist would encourage Jean to tell her story and empathize with her viewpoint to foster a therapeutic alliance. The mental health specialist would ask Jean to discuss her understanding of the negative consequences of alcohol use and assess her level of insight into her situation and whether she is in denial. It would be valuable to provide reassurance that help is available and that change happens with commitment.

The family would be involved early and often in treatment to lend support and insight, since treatment without their involvement has little hope of success. In Jean's case, the family could be an important part in healing unresolved grief. It would also be helpful to develop a substance abuse history of the extended family, since relatives with abuse issues increase the risk of addiction. A referral to Alcoholics Anonymous' teen program Alateen is for teens who've been affected by someone else's drinking, not teen alcoholics. Alateen can provide Jean with education and continued encouragement for abstinence. The early stages of abstinence require considerable support. The therapist will make clear that occasional relapses are possible and need to be seen as "human slips," not "failures" that confirm Jean's sense of low self-worth.

A therapist would continue to work with Jean and her family to prevent relapse and work through temporary relapses if they occur. Sessions would continually review the reasons for the recovery process; provide support, reassurance, encouragement, and praise for ongoing work; and explore for insight into the roots of the addiction. The therapist would encourage Jean to become involved in extracurricular social, athletic, or artistic activities with positive peer groups and to expand her interests. It would be important to identify and address family problems that may be complicating Jean's alcohol abuse. Family sessions could be used to teach communication skills and explore underlying family dysfunctions (such as an inability to express feelings) that may be related to the addictive behavior.

Regarding depression, a combination of cognitive-behavioral therapy, medication, and family therapy is the standard treatment. Significant depressive symptoms in teenagers can be treated with medication. They can be likened to a cast on a broken arm—a temporary support that promotes healing. Any medication for minors must be carefully monitored, given the ongoing physical and psychological development of young people.

In cognitive-behavioral therapy, there is an attempt to change depression-producing beliefs and attitudes to healthier, more realistic ones. Behaviors that produce pleasure and fulfillment are also encouraged. Many depressed adolescents define their life situation in global terms like "nothing is working out" or "I can't do anything right." Depressed youth tend to conclude the worst, dwell on negative details, and devalue the positive, especially when they have overly critical parents. Cognitive-behavioral therapy seeks to stop or modify these pessimistic "automatic thoughts" that people use to define themselves, their environment, and the future. If these beliefs go unrecognized and unchallenged, such distorted thinking will result in continued depression. Usually treatment involves self-monitoring of mood and activities, often in the form of keeping a daily log.

CONCLUSION

Jean is fortunate to have a psychologically minded pastor who was prepared to connect her with a specialized mental health professional who has the training and experience to help her effectively. Jean also has several factors going for her that point toward a long-term positive outcome. Importantly, she has the motivation to change and has responded well to treatment. In addition, she has the valuable support of her family and church community.

HELPFUL BOOKS

MacLachlan, Malcolm, and Caroline Smyth. 2004. *Binge Drinking and Youth Culture.* Dublin, UK: Liffey Press.

Preston, John. 2004. *You Can Beat Depression: A Guide to Prevention and Recovery.* San Luis Obispo: Impact Publishers.

Rogers, Peter D., and Lea Goldstein. 2002. *Drugs and Your Kid: How to Tell If Your Child Has a Drug/Alcohol Problem and What to Do About It.* Oakland: New Harbinger.

Rowatt, G. Wade. 1989. *Pastoral Care with Adolescents in Crisis.* Louisville: Westminster John Knox.

Schaefer, Dick. 1998. *Choices & Consequences: What to Do When a Teenager Uses Alcohol/Drugs.* Center City, Minn.: Hazelden Foundation.

Stone, Howard. 2008. *Crisis Counseling.* 3d ed. Creative Pastoral Care and Counseling. Minneapolis: Fortress Press.

Stone, Howard. 2007. *Defeating Depression: Real Help for You and Those Who Love You.* Minneapolis: Augsburg.

Weaver, Andrew J., John D. Preston, and Leigh W. Jerome. 1999. *Counseling Troubled Teens and Their Families: A Handbook for Pastors and Youth Workers.* Nashville: Abingdon.

2

CASE STUDY #2:
THE ALCOHOLIC GAMBLER

"He began to crave alcohol and betting."

Mark is a twenty-five-year-old single man who works as a certified public accountant and lives with his parents. He comes from a large family of three brothers and two sisters. Mark grew up in the Lutheran church but has not been involved in a congregation since he went off to college. He began drinking frequently in his undergraduate fraternity days.

A year ago Mark lost his driver's license for several months because he was arrested for driving while intoxicated. Soon thereafter he started drinking more and began to crave alcohol. Mark did manage to stay sober for a few weeks at a time with the encouragement of his family, but his sobriety did not last.

He became increasingly defensive about his drinking and began lying about it. Mark rationalized his excessive use of alcohol, blaming it on stress at work. Driving home one night after an evening at a casino gambling and drinking, he lost control of his car and ended up in the hospital in critical condition.

Mark displayed several of the key signs of a person who is addicted to alcohol. He continued to drink, despite serious problems resulting from its use. He developed a tolerance to alcohol and needed increasing amounts to achieve the desired effect. Mark frequently consumed more beverages over longer periods of time than intended and craved the anesthetic effects of alcohol. And, he had made several unsuccessful attempts to control its use.

He also showed signs of being a person with an addiction to gambling. Mark began to lose large amounts of money at the local casino. He sought the "high" of wagering increasing amounts of money and began to "chase" the losses of one day with increased betting the next day.

The time Mark spent in the hospital gave him a month of sobriety and a chance to reflect seriously on his life. He formed a solid bond with the hospital chaplain, Rev. Vince Judson, who listened to him and responded empathically, building trust in their relationship. Effective pastoral counseling, combined with the gravity of his injuries, moved Mark from denial of his alcoholism and gambling problem, to a consideration of how he could do something about his addictions, to finally reaching out for help. Chaplain Judson recognized that Mark's new attitude was a window of opportunity and that action needed to be taken. The chaplain, family members, Mark, and his physician discussed several treatment options.

RESPONSE TO VIGNETTE

The intensive outpatient treatment that Mark chose combines a number of alcohol treatment methods: client education, group therapy, Alcoholics Anonymous (AA) meetings, the prescription drug Antabuse, and pastoral counseling. Improving relationships and promoting good communication skills has been shown to be an important goal of treatment with individuals affected by alcoholism.

Mark and his family members are seen together to help them build teamwork and collaborative support for his sobriety, enhance relationships, increase positive feelings, and learn effective communication skills. The therapist emphasizes structured listening and speaking techniques to minimize the blaming, hostility, and avoidance that often occur in alcoholic family systems. Abstinence and acceptance of the disease of alcoholism are emphasized. Education helps instill new attitudes toward alcoholism—that it is an illness with recognizable signs and, like other diseases, it is treatable.

A common feature of alcohol dependence is a warped perception of reality. Group therapy and twelve-step groups can provide accurate feedback, lessen shame, and reduce isolation. A common problem for those in recovery is how to fill the time that was previously used for alcohol consumption. Planning and engaging in shared enjoyable times that do not involve alcohol is essential.

Mark made a sobriety contract, and he now takes Antabuse daily at an agreed upon time with the support of his family. Antabuse, which is widely used in the treatment of alcoholism, alters the way the body uses an enzyme that affects the normal metabolism of alcohol. It creates adverse effects for anyone drinking alcohol, including: a throbbing in the head and neck, nausea, vomiting, sweating, weakness, and vertigo. Antabuse cannot cure alcoholism, but it is a strong deterrent to impulsive drinking. Continued sobriety can help Mark build confidence that he can stop drinking, giving his family and friends assurance that will build trust and decrease conflict about alcohol over time.

Through ongoing contact Rev. Judson provides support, reassurance, and praise for Mark's recovery work. He encourages cooperation with the treatment and perseverance in difficult times. The chaplain helps Mark renew his connection with God through regular prayer and spiritual reflection. Chaplain Judson also helped him reconnect with the Lutheran church of his childhood.

The Lutheran pastor, Rev. Anne Larson, is able to provide an ongoing relationship. She was prepared through her clinical pastoral education training to recognize the early signs of a relapse, thereby preventing or minimizing its negative effects. Reverend Larson can help him gain perspective when a relapse occurs and reframe it as an opportunity to learn. It is a reality of human nature that people will backslide, especially in the first year of abstinence, and a plan to deal with relapse is a realistic goal. Pastors have professional training and experience in using the powerful resources of faith, hope, and compassion to help sustain the healing process. The underlying cause of an addiction such as alcoholism is often a spiritual crisis, which can be a turning point that will help a person transform the way in which he or she understands life, as well as renewing meaning in life.

Treatment for pathological gambling is most often patterned after the treatment of alcohol and other drug addictions (Petry, 2002). Like alcohol abusers, compulsive gamblers tend to deny the problem and avoid finding help. Gamblers Anonymous (GA), like AA, is a twelve-step program that encourages members to admit their problem and gives group support to help participants gain control over gambling. GA members learn to recognize the loss of reality caused by compulsive gambling and confront their own distorted thinking. Family members can join Gam-Anon, which is modeled after Al-Anon, for group support. Mark will continue to need support to help him stop living in the fantasy world of gambling addiction and confront the reality of the consequences of his self-destructive behavior.

DIAGNOSTIC CRITERIA

Alcohol dependence is characterized by a group of symptoms indicating that an individual continues to use alcohol despite significant resulting problems. Persons suffering alcohol dependence have a pattern of compulsive use, usually leading to tolerance and withdrawal, and "craving" for alcohol exists. According to the *Diagnostic and Statistical Manual of Mental Disorders* criteria (4th edition, Text Revision, 2000), at least three of the following symptoms must be present at the same time over a twelve-month period (APA, 2000):

- Tolerance has developed. This involves a need for increased amounts of alcohol to achieve the desired effect or the experience of diminished effects with continued use of the same amount.
- Withdrawal symptoms, such as physical discomfort, illness, or severe complications, are experienced by a person when alcohol is not available.
- Alcohol is frequently consumed in larger amounts or over longer periods of time than intended.
- There is a recurrent desire or unsuccessful attempts to control or cut down on alcohol use.
- A lot of time is devoted to activities related to obtaining alcohol, using it, or recovering from its effects.
- Important social, occupational, or recreational activities are reduced or stopped as a result of alcohol consumption.
- Alcohol is used in spite of persistent psychological or physical problems caused or exacerbated by its use.

The marked increase in places and methods to wager over the past fifteen years has been accompanied by an increased frequency of gambling addiction. *Pathological gambling* is a "persistent and recurrent maladaptive gambling behavior" that continues despite adverse consequences which are disruptive to one's life (APA, 2000). Approximately 2.5 million adults in North America (between 1.6 percent and 1.9 percent) may suffer from pathological gambling, with an additional 5.3 million adults (3.9 percent) at risk for the disorder (Shaffer et al., 1999). For comparison, the rate of cocaine abuse or dependence is estimated to be 0.2 percent (Regier et al., 1990).

Similar to alcohol abuse, the characteristics of pathological gambling include preoccupation with gambling, loss of control, tolerance, withdrawal-like symptoms, and cycles of abstinence and relapse (APA, 2000). The term *problem gambler* is used to describe those who have some degree of gambling difficulties but do not meet the full diagnostic criteria for pathological gambling (Shaffer et al., 1999). Pathological and problem gamblers are more likely than recreational gamblers and nongamblers to have experienced an episode of depression, lost their job, been arrested, filed for bankruptcy, and/or to have a substance disorder (National Research Council, 1999).

Many studies have found a strong relationship between alcohol abuse and problem or pathological gambling. A survey of over three thousand adults found that among a combined group of problem and pathological gamblers, 44.5 percent met lifetime criteria for alcohol abuse or dependency (Cunningham-Williams et al., 1998). These rates of substance-use disorders in problem and pathological gamblers are far higher than rates found in non-problem gamblers.

TREATMENT WITHIN THE FAITH COMMUNITY

There is scientific evidence that, across the lifespan, individuals involved in nurturing, nonpunitive religion are less likely than the general population to abuse alcohol and other substances, take part in the excessive use of addictive substances, and suffer the adverse effects of dependence (Larson et al., 1998). Religious practice and strength of religion in the family are inversely associated with anti-social behavior in young people, including fewer drug and alcohol problems (Weaver et al., 1999).

One way that churches can help persons in recovery from addictions is to provide space and support for twelve-step self-help groups that provide a spiritually based supportive fellowship in which a major source of strength is a member's Higher Power. In 1989 it was estimated that ten to fifteen million people in the United States participated in a half-million twelve-step or other mutual help groups (Goldsmith, 1989). Active involvement in twelve-step programs like AA, GA, and Narcotics Anonymous are helpful for persons with addictions. The programs work equally well for addicts of all economic and educational levels (Miller and

Verinis, 1995). These groups can function as caring environments in which members feel safe and secure, offering a natural bridge in the process of reconnecting with the community when addicts are tempted to withdraw and isolate themselves.

Researchers have begun to find that religious involvement can be a protective factor against gambling problems. In a nationwide sample of U.S. adults, religious attendance was inversely associated with the risk of problem gambling (Hoffman, 2000). In a statewide survey, sociologists at the University of Texas found that religious attendance and belief in the Bible were inversely associated with the frequency of playing the state lottery, as well as the amount of money spent on it (Ellison and Nybroten, 1999). Among individuals in Nevada, the frequency of gambling and the amount of money gambled was discovered to be inversely related to the level of importance of religion for the person and the frequency of their attendance at religious services (Diaz, 2000).

TREATMENT BY MENTAL HEALTH SPECIALISTS

Alcoholism is a major social problem that usually goes untreated. Forty-three percent of American families indicate they have a family member with an alcohol problem (Dann, 2002), while only a small minority of them receive treatment (Edwards and Steinglass, 1995). Substance abuse results in considerable costs for the sufferer, his or her family, and society—lost jobs, family disruption, financial instability, accidental injury, and death.

A key question for clergy dealing with persons with alcohol and drug problems is when to help. Mark had a rapid conversion after his life-threatening automobile accident that moved him quickly from denial that he had a drinking problem to acceptance to the point of seeking help. Most addicted persons change much more slowly.

The psychologist William Miller has divided the process into stages (Miller and Jackson, 1995). It begins with "precontemplation" when a person is not interested in change and moves to "contemplation" when an individual begins to consider it, wavering between favoring and resisting action. The third stage, in which a person acknowledges the problem and recognizes the need for action, is called "determination." At this critical point where motivation is reached and a decision to act is made, immediate intervention is required.

It is important for clergy and other religious professionals to prepare a list of community resources for addiction problems before being faced with the immediate need to assist someone. Develop appropriate plans of action with mental health colleagues before an emergency occurs.

An assessment will need to be made as to whether inpatient detoxification is required for individuals who are alcohol dependent. The following indicate inpatient care may be the treatment of choice:

- alcohol use is associated with imminent danger to self or another;
- severe mental illness (e.g., major depression, psychosis, post-traumatic stress disorder);
- failure in previous attempts at outpatient treatment; or
- the lack of a support system.

Cognitive and behavioral therapies are often used to treat persons with addictions, including gambling. This method seeks to reframe thinking patterns and change habits that promote gambling behavior. Mark would be taught to identify and record situations that bring on the compulsion to wager and to recognize the distorted thinking that he can win against the odds. These methods have been tested and shown to work in several populations. In a study of Canadian men who entered a course of treatment for pathological gambling using a cognitive-behavioral model that included relapse prevention training, 86 percent were no longer gambling a year after treatment (Sylvain et al., 1997).

CONCLUSION

It is helpful to assess a person's assets when developing a pastoral care evaluation. Several strengths point to a positive prognosis for Mark. He has a supportive extended family and pastoral team who are actively interested in his welfare and willing to work with him on his addiction. He also has good vocational skills, a college education, resilience, and the capability of insight into his illness. Mark will need help to focus on his strengths, successes, and resources during his recovery. Alcohol and gambling addictions are long-term issues that will require all of his psychological and spiritual resources.

HELPFUL BOOKS

Ciarrocchi, Joseph W. 2001. *Counseling Problem Gamblers and Their Families*. San Diego: Academic Press.

Clinebell, Howard. 1998. *Understanding and Counseling: Persons with Alcohol, Drug, and Behavioral Addictions*. Nashville: Abingdon.

Dann, Bucky. 2002. *Addiction: Pastoral Response*. Nashville: Abingdon.

Federman, Edward, and Charles Drebing. 2000. *Don't Leave It to Chance: A Guide for Families of Problem Gamblers*. Oakland: New Harbinger.

Ketcham, Katherine, Arthur P. Ciaramicoli, William F. Asbury, and Mel Schulstad. 2000. *Beyond the Influence: Understanding and Defeating Alcoholism*. New York: Bantam.

Perkinson, Robert R. 2003. *The Gambling Addiction Patient Workbook*. New York: Sage.

Ladouceur, Robert, Caroline Sylvain, Claude Boutin, and Celine Doucet. 2002. *Understanding and Treating the Pathological Gambler*. New York: John Wiley.

3

CASE STUDY #3:
THE TRAUMATIZED VETERAN

"Alcohol helped him forget."

Alex joined the Marine Corps after high school in response to the 9/11 attacks. He came home to his fiancée, Janet, and his family after two tours of duty in Iraq. His unit was involved in numerous combat operations and several of Alex's close buddies did not survive. He witnessed the horror of dozens of murdered men, women, and children lying in a roadside ditch. Alex appeared to be perfectly normal when he returned. Over time he became more and more irritable, however, and Janet recognized he was no longer his friendly self. He was emotionally withdrawn from her, family members, and old friends. When Janet and his family tried to talk to him about the changes they saw, Alex became angry and said that nothing was wrong and he did not want to talk. Horrible nightmares began, keeping him up half the night. He began to drink heavily in an attempt to make himself forget the horrors of Iraq. After Alex went on a week-long binge, Janet became frantic and sought out Reverend King for guidance.

RESPONSE TO VIGNETTE

After listening to Janet's concerns about Alex, it became clear to the pastor that the alcohol problem and psychological trauma must be addressed. Reverend King consulted with a social worker colleague who had expertise in alcohol abuse. They decided that the best course of action was a group intervention, involving the social worker, pastor, fiancée, family members, and friends, where they would try to help Alex recognize the extent of his alcohol problem and how his post-traumatic stress disorder (PTSD) was related to the substance abuse (see PTSD symptoms below, p. 22, and the glossary). Alcohol abusers, like Alex, usually do not know they are out of control. They need feedback through a nonjudgmental process to confront the effect of their alcohol abuse and PTSD symptoms on others. The goal of the intervention was for Alex to accept the reality of his addiction and psychological trauma and to make a commitment to seek help. No group intervention should be undertaken without advice and counsel of a professional experienced in the process. As a result of the intervention, Alex agreed to seek treatment through the Veterans Administration (VA).

War is a life-threatening experience that involves witnessing and sometimes engaging in terrifying and gruesome acts of violence. It is normal for Alex to react to war's psychic trauma with feelings of fear, anger, grief, repulsion, helplessness, and horror, as well as with emotional numbness and disbelief. Many veterans are psychologically unable to leave behind the trauma of war when they return home. They struggle with a variety of severe problems that neither they nor their families, friends, or communities know how to address or understand (Weaver et al., 2003).

Combat veterans, like Alex, may think that they are going crazy or that there is something wrong with them, since some others who were at the same place do not seem to have the same problems. Because thinking about a trauma and feeling endangered is upsetting, people who have experienced combat generally want to avoid all reminders. Survivors may not know what to do to get better. As one might expect, the most important risk factor for PTSD among veterans is the level of exposure to traumatic events during war (Weaver et al., 2003).

Stress reactions can create sleep disturbances, irritability, intrusive painful reexperiencing of events, restricted emotional capacity, and impairments of memory and problem-solving capabilities (APA, 2000). Long-term stress reactions may include depression, chronic anxiety, and the symptoms of PTSD. These symptoms include:

- reexperiencing events (nightmares, intrusive thoughts);
- avoidance (staying away from situations that remind a veteran of what happened);
- a variety of indications of hyperarousal (sleep disturbance, an exaggerated startle response, irritability); and
- restriction in the capacity to experience and express feelings (APA, 2000).

Perhaps the most perplexing symptom for relatives and friends to understand is psychological numbness: a withdrawal of affection and avoidance of close emotional ties with family members, friends, and colleagues. These responses can cause or exacerbate marital, vocational, or substance abuse problems (Figley, 1989).

A common response to PTSD is to self-medicate with alcohol or other drugs to alleviate the distressing feelings and thoughts. Substance use problems are common in individuals with PTSD, occurring in an estimated 50 to 85 percent of those with the disorder (Kessler et al., 1995). Data indicates that the degree of exposure to combat is specifically associated with increased alcohol abuse (Kulka et al., 1990). Unfortunately, the use of alcohol and other substances can actually increase the likelihood of symptoms associated with PTSD (Coffey et al., 2006). It is essential that Alex be treated for the alcohol abuse to help manage the PTSD symptoms.

DIAGNOSTIC CRITERIA

Alex is a binge drinker, which is defined as having five or more drinks per drinking occasion over the course of thirty days. A national survey involving more than seventy thousand people found that almost one in five of those aged 12 to 20 are binge drinkers (SAMHSA, 2005).

Alcohol abuse has as its basic feature a pattern characterized by negative, recurrent, and significant consequences related to repeated use. This diagnosis requires only one of the following criteria in the past twelve months (APA, 2000):

1. Recurrent alcohol use results in a failure to fulfill major obligations at home or work (such as repeated neglect of school responsibilities).
2. Repeated use of alcohol in situations in which use is known to be physically hazardous.
3. Recurrent alcohol-related legal problems.
4. Continued use despite having persistent or recurrent social or interpersonal problems resulting from the effects of the alcohol (such as arguments with friends or family members about the consequences of using the alcohol).

Post-traumatic stress disorder (PTSD) is a significant public health problem. About 8 percent of Americans have PTSD at some point in their life, making it the fourth most common psychiatric disorder (Kessler et al., 1995). PTSD is not a sign of being "emotionally weak" or "mentally ill." Virtually anyone exposed to the "shock effect" of extreme stress will find their ordinary coping processes are overwhelmed. PTSD is diagnosed when a person responds with intense fear, helplessness, or horror to a traumatic experience that involves actual or threatened death, serious injury, or a threat to the physical well-being of self or others (APA, 2000). A traumatic event is reexperienced in specific ways, such as recurrent and intrusive distressing recollections or dreams of the event. Additionally, a person often persistently avoids situations associated with a trauma and has emotional numbness in general. Often there is hypervigilance and irritability. PTSD becomes the diagnosis when these symptoms persist for more than one month.

TREATMENT WITHIN THE FAITH COMMUNITY

Unfortunately, many soldiers returning from the wars in Iraq and Afghanistan are not getting the mental health treatment they need. In July of 2004, the prestigious *New England Journal of Medicine* published a study by researchers at Walter Reed Army Medical Center. They found that up to 17 percent of the combat veterans returning from Iraq had PTSD, but only 40 percent of those with PTSD sought psychological care. Stigma associated with seeking mental health treatment was the greatest single barrier to obtaining the help needed (Hoge et al., 2004). If the same pattern unfolds that tragically affected Vietnam-era veterans and these PTSD sufferers do not obtain appropriate help, many will become unnecessarily and tragically addicted to drugs and/or alcohol.

Pastors and churches are in a valuable position to help with these problems. In psychological trauma, an individual's sense of order and continuity in life is shattered, and questions of meaning and purpose abound. Studies have shown that religious faith is a primary coping strategy for many people, including recovering combat veterans suffering from psychological trauma (Weaver et al., 2003). In addition to offering the natural social support of community, faith can provide a suffering person with a framework to find meaning and perspective through a source greater than self, and it can give a sense of control over feelings of helplessness. Research has found that nurturing, nonpunitive faith can enhance well-being and facilitate emotional recovery for many traumatized individuals (Weaver et al., 2003).

Clergy are called upon to play a variety of roles as they help trauma survivors move through the healing process. Pastors are accessible and trusted, and through wise counsel they can aid in removing the sigma from mental health care. Clergy are often in long-term relationships with individuals and their families, providing ongoing contacts in which they can observe changes in behavior that can assist in the assessment and treatment of veterans with PTSD. Pastors are also in a position in which they can refer veterans to mental health specialists and other support systems available through faith communities (Weaver et al., 2003).

One way that congregations of faith can help persons in recovery from addictions is to provide space and support for twelve-step self-help groups that provide a spiritually based supportive fellowship. About 9 percent of American adults have attended an Alcoholics Anonymous (AA) meeting, and 13 percent have attended a twelve-step program of some type (Room and Greenfield, 1993). Many recovering persons find it helpful to attend twelve-step meetings in addition to their professional treatment.

TREATMENT BY MENTAL HEALTH SPECIALISTS

Alcohol abuse is a significant public health problem that usually goes untreated. It is estimated that 2.7 percent of Americans twelve years of age or older experience problems associated with alcohol and substance abuse that require treatment, although only a small minority of them receive it (Edwards and Steinglass, 1995). Such abuse results in considerable costs for the sufferer, his or her family, and society—lost jobs, family disruption, financial instability, accidental injury, and death.

Cognitive-behavioral therapy has proven to be an effective treatment for many patients. Environment strongly influences an individual's thinking and behavior, so cognitive-behavioral therapy teaches new ways of acting and thinking in response to one's surroundings. For example, persons are taught to avoid situations that lead to drug use and to practice skills to say no to offers of alcohol. This approach is aimed at helping patients strengthen their commitment to abstinence, deal effectively with urges and risky situations, recognize and change irrational thoughts, manage negative moods, and increase social support.

Individual therapy is also an important part of treatment. Individual sessions allow the therapists to obtain histories and develop structured treatment plans. In addition, the individual sessions give clients an opportunity to discuss matters that were not covered adequately in groups. Relapse prevention should be a part of any drug treatment program and has proven to help people avoid returning to alcohol abuse.

It is important that clergy be knowledgeable about the services provided by the Veterans Administration (VA). The VA medical centers make available a network of more than one hundred specialized programs for persons with PTSD, working closely with the centers operated by VA Readjustment Counseling Service (see the resource section, below). Teams offer outpatient education, evaluation, and counseling for the combined problems of PTSD and substance abuse.

Close relationships are almost always adversely affected by PTSD, which, along with other stress-related problems, can affect an entire family. Many times couples or family therapy can help a family cope with a veteran's stress-related problems. Treatment may include stress-reduction and relaxation techniques that can help all members of the family with the healing process. Therapy might also address the structure of the family and the way that members interact (Figley, 1989).

CONCLUSION

Alex is fortunate that Janet cared enough to seek Reverend King's advice. The pastor already had established a mental health network which provided him with the resources to set up the intervention during which Alex agreed to seek treatment. With the support of all those involved in the intervention and the treatment provided by the Veterans Administration, there is the likelihood of a positive outcome.

HELPFUL BOOKS

Allen, Jon. 1995. *Coping with Trauma: A Guide to Self-Understanding.* Washington, D.C.: American Psychiatric Press.

Friedman, Marvin. 2000. *Post Traumatic Stress Disorder: The Latest Assessment and Treatment Strategies.* Kansas City, Mo.: Compact Clinicians.

Hansel, Sarah, Ann Steidle, Grace Zaczek, and Ron Zaczek. 1994. *Soldiers' Heart: Survivors' Views of Combat Trauma.* Lutherville, Md.: Sidran Press.

Herman, J. L. 1992. *Trauma and Recovery.* New York: Basic Books.

Matsakis, Aphrodite. 1992. *I Can't Get Over It: A Handbook for Trauma Survivors.* Oakland: New Harbinger.

Michel, Christopher P. 2005. *The Military Advantage: A Comprehensive Guide to Your Military & Veterans Benefits.* New York: Simon & Schuster.

Tick, Edward. 2005. *War and the Soul: Healing Our Nation's Veterans from Post-traumatic Stress Disorder.* New York: Quest Books.

Weaver, Andrew Laura Flannelly, and John Preston. 2003. *Counseling Survivors of Traumatic Events: A Handbook for Pastors and Other Helping Professionals.* Nashville: Abingdon.

4

CASE STUDY #4: THE GRIEVING OLDER WOMAN

"The grief and loneliness has become almost unbearable."

Ruth, age seventy-four, has lived alone for the six months since her husband died after a prolonged illness. She cared for him during the last two years of his life. This experience was difficult for both of them since they were very close. Since his death, the grief and loneliness has become almost unbearable for Ruth. Usually a weekly churchgoer, she has reduced her worship attendance to about once a month since Bill's death and for the past couple of months has completely stopped going. Seeing her church friends with their husbands by their side reminds her of how much she misses him. Also, she feels uncomfortable as a single person trying to socialize with the couples with whom she and her husband had done things in the past. She simply does not have the energy or motivation to get up and go to church anymore.

Ruth and her husband had always had a couple glasses of wine in the evening to help relax them and often drank alcohol with friends socially. After her husband died, she discovered that drinking wine helped to numb her painful feelings and also helped her to fall asleep. Ruth gradually increased the number of glasses of wine from two to four per evening. Although she was able to fall asleep better, she found herself waking up about 2:00 or 3:00 in the morning, unable to go back to sleep. This caused her to feel tired throughout the day. Ruth asked her doctor for a sleeping aid, and he prescribed low dose Valium to help her to rest and reduce the anxiety and fear that she reported feeling when she was home alone. Lately, she had begun taking an additional Valium tablet or two in the morning to "calm her nerves."

Over the past several months, Ruth has become more and more unsteady on her feet, falling a couple of times, and one time breaking her wrist. She also had a fender-bender recently while driving, when she failed to notice that the car in front of her had stopped. Her memory and concentration seemed to be getting increasingly worse, but when her daughter asked about it, she denied any problem and simply attributed it to her age. When she saw her doctor, he noticed that her blood pressure was up and that she had lost some weight. When he asked her about her drinking, she admitted to having a couple of glasses of wine with her dinner, but said she never drank before 6:00 at night and claimed that it helped to increase her appetite. Her physician encouraged her to cut down to just one glass with dinner, but she found it difficult to follow his advice.

Not having seen her in worship for several months, and being in the area visiting another member, Pastor David decided to pay her a visit. It was 3:00 P.M. when Ruth answered the door, dressed in a stained nightgown partially covered by her robe. Her hair was messy, and she appeared very tired. Surprised, she cautiously greeted David and, with some hesitation, invited him in. He warmly greeted her and walked into her apartment. He immediately noticed a strong odor in the room—a mixture of urine, body odor, and rotting garbage. He also observed that clothes were strewn about, dishes and papers were piled on the table, and the garbage pail was overflowing. Ruth apologized for the way the room looked and invited David to sit down on the part of the couch she cleared off. Once they were seated, David remarked that he missed seeing her in church and inquired how she had been doing since Bill died. "Not so good," she replied. "I miss him terribly." And she began to choke up.

Ruth is abusing alcohol and is experiencing some of the physical, emotional, and social effects of heavy alcohol use. She may also be dependent on a benzodiazepine (Valium), which has central nervous system effects similar to those of alcohol. In addition to her substance abuse, Ruth may have a depressive disorder or be experiencing a complicated grief reaction.

Ruth is consistently having four or more glasses of wine per night and is beginning to experience physical symptoms of excessive alcohol intake (problems with balance and falling, difficulties concentrating, increase in blood pressure). Approximately five ounces of wine is considered one drink (which is equivalent to 1.5 ounces of distilled spirits or twelve ounces of beer). Heavy drinking is defined as having three or more drinks per day, while moderate alcohol consumption is defined as two drinks per day for men and one drink per day for women. The National Institute on Alcohol

Abuse and Addictions (NIAAA) recommends that persons over age sixty-five consume no more than one drink per day due to physiological changes with age that increase blood alcohol levels (O'Connor & Schottenfeld, 1998).

Studies indicate that almost two-thirds of community-dwelling elderly adults drink alcohol, and 13 percent of men and 2 percent of women are heavy drinkers (Mirand and Welte, 1996). Approximately 6 to 11 percent of older patients admitted to the hospital have symptoms of alcoholism, which is also true for 20 percent of hospitalized older psychiatric patients and 14 percent of older patients seen in emergency rooms (Council on Scientific Affairs, 1996).

Most studies that have followed younger or middle-aged adults into later life report little change in alcohol consumption as people age. If change does occur, alcohol use usually decreases due to fewer social opportunities to drink, less money to purchase alcohol, health problems that prevent use, and less toleration of its effects.

However, Ruth has late-onset alcoholism, since her heavy drinking started after she turned seventy years of age. About one-third of elderly alcoholics began their heavy drinking after age sixty-five (Council on Scientific Affairs, 1996). The more prevalent form of alcoholism among older adults is the early-onset variety (up to 70 percent of cases). Those with early-onset alcoholism are more likely to have a history of antisocial behavior and a family history of alcoholism. Socioeconomic status generally is lower and family estrangement more common among early-onset alcoholics (Stinson et al., 1989). In contrast, late-onset alcoholics have higher education levels and higher income, and drinking tends to be precipitated or worsened by stressful life events, such as bereavement or retirement (LaGreca et al., 1988). Retirement communities are known to have a relatively high prevalence of late-onset alcohol problems, since social drinking tends to be the norm (Atkinson et al., 1990).

Besides alcohol abuse (and possibly alcohol dependence), Ruth is abusing tranquilizers (benzodiazepines), since she is taking more than the dose of Valium recommended by her physician. She may be treating symptoms of alcohol withdrawal in the morning (tremulousness, nervousness) by taking the extra dose of Valium. Studies indicate that approximately 15 percent of older alcoholics are also abusing or dependent on other drugs such as benzodiazepines (Finlayson et al., 1988).

Finally, it sounds as if Ruth is having a complicated grief reaction and also may be experiencing a major depressive disorder. She is tired, not sleeping well, losing weight, socially withdrawn, and is feeling painful depressive symptoms. As noted in Case #1 and Case #3, depressive disorders tend to co-occur with alcohol abuse (Adams, 1998; Welte, 1998). Data from the National Longitudinal Alcohol Epidemiologic Survey indicates that elderly alcoholics are three times more likely than elders without alcoholism to have a major depressive disorder (Grant and Harford, 1995).

RESPONSE TO VIGNETTE

Pastor David quickly realizes that things are not going well for Ruth. She describes how painful living without Bill has been, and admits to drinking a bit more than she should and taking extra Valium because of her worsening "nerves." From the conversation, David determines that there is a good chance that Ruth is suffering from alcoholism, excessive sedative use, depression, and social isolation, and that she needs both professional help and support from loved ones. David encourages Ruth to call her only child (who lives several states away) to talk with her about what has been going on. He also urges Ruth to get an appointment as soon as possible with her physician and offers to go with her to the doctor's office.

David will want to ensure that her physician gets Ruth connected with mental health professionals who can treat her alcoholism and the problems that led up to it. Finally, he will eventually want to encourage her gently to get involved in the church, attending worship regularly and participating in Bible study or prayer groups in order to develop relationships that will help provide support and meet other needs. David will want to follow up with Ruth to verify that she is getting the help she needs and later getting the support from the church that will be essential to her long-term recovery.

DIAGNOSTIC CRITERIA

Ruth fulfills the criteria for alcohol abuse, and possibly even alcohol dependence, although we do not know enough to determine this (see criteria for alcohol abuse and dependence on p. 40-41). The symptoms favoring alcohol dependence are that she has increased her alcohol use (suggesting development of tolerance), has failed in attempts to reduce that intake (despite recommendations by her physician), and may be having withdrawal symptoms in the morning that she is self-medicating with Valium.

Signs of alcoholism in the elderly, many of which Ruth has, include:

- problems with memory and concentration;
- difficulty caring for self and keeping the environment clean and safe;
- not following through with medical appointments and treatment;
- unstable or poorly controlled hypertension, accidents, injuries, or falls;
- frequent visits to the emergency room;
- gastrointestinal problems that may be associated with weight loss;
- unexpected delirium during hospitalization (due to alcohol withdrawal);
- estrangement from family, especially with the early-onset variety.

The most common screening tool used by medical professionals to detect alcoholism is the CAGE test. It asks a person if he/she ever feels the need to Cut down on their alcohol consumption; whether he/she gets Annoyed when people criticize or question his/her use of alcohol; whether he/she feels Guilty about his/her drinking habits; and whether he/she needs an Eye-opener in the mornings. A positive response to any one of the above four questions indicates an alcohol problem. Ruth was told to cut down on her drinking by her physician, and she reports being nervous and anxious in the mornings (although instead of drinking, she takes Valium).

TREATMENT WITHIN THE FAITH COMMUNITY

For Ruth, who lives alone and has no nearby relatives to help her, the faith community will need to assume the role that family members would ordinarily perform, unless her daughter takes on these tasks. This includes the following:

- Monitoring and helping her to get medical attention for any decline in her cognition or self-care;
- Providing information, if known, about her recent and lifetime drinking problems;
- Participating in confrontation as needed (helping her to recognize that she has a problem and needs help);
- Supporting her during detoxification and long-term alcohol rehabilitation and treatment;
- Helping coordinate community services and resources;
- Helping to make decisions for Ruth if her cognitive impairment worsens so that she is unable to process information, weigh consequences, or communicate decisions (although her health-care power of attorney would be triggered if she had one, and this may be held by her daughter).

Besides acting as a surrogate family, the faith community can provide the support that Ruth will need over the long term to prevent relapse into drinking, excessive benzodiazepine use, or falling into isolation and depression. Her church can provide the loving contacts that will meet her need for long-term social support, companionship, spiritual encouragement, and opportunities for volunteer work that could make a big difference in Ruth's future recovery.

TREATMENT BY MENTAL HEALTH SPECIALISTS

After detoxification (possibly as an inpatient in the hospital), Ruth will need further treatment in an inpatient alcohol rehabilitation program, day treatment program, individual outpatient therapy (for both alcoholism and depression), and/or involvement in community-based groups such as Alcoholics Anonymous (AA). Delays from the time of detoxification to enrollment in an alcohol rehabilitation program should be avoided, since this will reduce the likelihood of successful completion of such programs. Cognitive-behavioral therapy, interpersonal psychotherapy, and supportive counseling have all been effective in treating depression in older adults. Antidepressant medications may also need to be prescribed and monitored. Risk for suicide should also be assessed.

Late-onset alcoholics have been found to do better in elder-specific alcohol treatment programs than with mixed-age programs (Schonfeld and Dupree, 1995; Liberto et al., 1992). Therefore, finding an alcohol rehabilitation program that provides care specifically for elderly adults would be best for Ruth. Such programs, however, are not readily available.

Because they have greater resources and family support, late-onset alcoholics are more likely to complete treatment programs (elder-specific or not) and have better outcomes than early-onset alcoholics. One study of late-onset alcoholics that followed them over time found that 21 percent of subjects remained in stable remission at four years of follow-up, which was almost twice as likely as for early-onset alcoholics (Schutte et al., 1994). Although this means that only one of five late-onset alcoholics will have good outcomes, persons like Ruth, with the support of their pastor and faith community, stand a high chance of long-term remission.

In addition, some physically or cognitively frail elderly alcoholics may benefit from a comprehensive geriatric medical and psychiatric assessment (which might be done in a university-based clinic) and then referral to appropriate community resources for home care, nutritional programs, transportation, and/or other services. For elderly alcoholics with advanced dementia who have lost the ability to care for themselves, nursing home placement may be necessary. Because depression can sometimes mask itself as dementia, however, it is important that a psychiatric evaluation take place to rule out and/or treat depression (which, as we saw above, is three times more common in alcoholic than in nonalcoholic elderly persons).

CONCLUSION

Ruth has a number of strengths that favor a good long-term prognosis if she receives adequate treatment and support. She was married for many years in a stable relationship and was committed to her husband (caring for him during his last years of life). She was active in her church community for many years until she started to withdraw as a result of a complicated grief reaction, depression, and substance abuse. Her alcohol intake escalated only after the death of her husband, and in response to intense loneliness and grief. Whether or not she falls into the 20 percent of people who maintain a stable sobriety will depend in large part on the kind of support that she receives from her faith community and her reinvolvement in the congregation as an active member.

HELPFUL BOOKS

Graham, Kathryn, Sarah J. Saunders, and Margaret Cameron Coss Flower. 1995. *Addictions Treatment for Older Adults: Evaluation of an Innovative Client-Centered Approach.* Binghamton, N.Y.: Haworth.

Johnson, Vernon E. 1990. *I'll Quit Tomorrow: A Practical Guide to Alcoholism Treatment.* San Francisco: HarperCollins.

Lawton, Kristen, and David Oslin. 2001. *Alcohol Problems in Older Adults: Prevention and Management.* New York: Springer.

Salzman, Carl. 2000. *Psychiatric Medications for Older Adults: The Concise Guide.* New York: Guilford.

Sullender, Scott R. 1999. *Losses in Later Life: A New Way of Walking With God.* New York: Haworth.

Weaver, Andrew, and Howard Stone. 2005. *Reflections on Grief and Spiritual Growth.* Nashville: Abingdon.

5

CASE STUDY #5:
THE RETIRED DRINKER

"He stumbled outside the door."

It was John's seventieth birthday. His wife, Sarah, had planned a party for him to celebrate. His son, Bob, and daughter, Julie, and their spouses had arrived. Even their pastor, Todd, was there. Everything was to begin at 7:00 P.M., after John returned from doing some errands. They waited and waited, but he did not come home that night until almost 11:00. By the time he got home, everyone had left except Sarah and Todd. John stumbled outside the door, banging it with his shoulder, and then began fumbling with his keys, although the door was unlocked. When Sarah and Todd greeted him, they noticed a strong smell of alcohol on his breath. His hair was a bit disheveled, and his shirt had a large stain on it.

In a friendly voice Todd said, "Happy birthday, John," but Sarah was silent. John mumbled something and went to the bathroom. When he finished in there, he went into the bedroom and shut the door. Todd and Sarah retired to the kitchen. The pastor asked if everything was okay. Sarah said that things had not been going well since John retired two years earlier from his real estate business. After traveling in Europe and spending time in Hawaii, they settled down to a quiet and routine life. John grew bored, though, and had grown increasingly irritable. After a long and fulfilling career in business, the slowdown was hard for him. John had loved his work, especially the interactions with clients and colleagues. Now it was just him and Sarah at home.

Last year John had a heart attack and small stroke, which left him partially disabled. Because of this, he now takes several medications for his heart, blood pressure, and cholesterol. John has not coped well since the heart attack. For many years, he enjoyed a glass of bourbon or two with his supper, but over the past year he increased to two drinks before dinner and three to four more during the evening. He ended up falling asleep in his chair each night around 9:00 and after midnight would stumble into bed. Sarah noticed that he had also been having a drink or two after lunch and occasionally in the morning. She lamented that John and she had not had much of a relationship for many months.

Increasingly concerned about his alcohol consumption, Sarah asked him to stop drinking in the morning and afternoon and to limit himself to a couple of drinks with dinner, as was his earlier pattern. When she said anything about his drinking, though, John would become upset and tell her to leave him alone. His behavior was beginning to put a serious strain on their marriage, and Sarah was becoming increasingly uncomfortable with the situation. John seemed to be a completely different person than the man whom she married and had lived with for over forty years.

For the past couple of weeks, John had been leaving after dinner to "run errands." He would sometimes be gone for hours at a time, refusing to tell his wife where he had gone. Sarah had told John that she had something special planned for tonight, and he had promised to be home by 7:00. John's missing his own birthday party was the last straw for Sarah. She told Todd that she did not know how much longer she could take this and asked her pastor for help.

As noted in the last case, there are two general types of alcoholism in later life. The first involves a person who has used alcohol heavily and been dependent on it for many years (usually beginning in their twenties or thirties). "Early-onset" alcoholism describes about two-thirds of older alcoholics. This is the lifelong alcoholic who has simply survived into his or her later years. This person is often single, male, and may be of low socioeconomic status since drinking habits have interfered with education, work, and relationships.

The other type of late-life alcoholic is a person who may have used alcohol moderately in earlier years, but begins to increase consumption in later life in response to challenging circumstances or changes in health and mobility. In this "late-onset" type, alcohol is used to cope with situational stressors. Unfortunately, drinking only compounds those stresses and often contributes to worsening health problems. If an older alcoholic is married, the spouse or other family members who live in the household are often on the receiving end of the drinker's anger and frustrations. Late-onset alcoholism describes about one-third of older alcoholics. Rates of depression and suicide are high among alcoholics, especially the late-onset variety, after they have driven away concerned family members. Of all groups in the population, it is the older divorced white male with chronic illness and alcohol problems who is at highest risk for completed suicide. Having a caring spouse in the same household, then, may make the difference between life and death for John.

RESPONSE TO VIGNETTE

That evening, Todd had an opportunity to talk with Sarah. What has this situation been like for her? Does she need to see a counselor to help her deal with her feelings? If so, Todd can encourage her to see someone and perhaps get involved in an Al-Anon group. Al-Anon is an organization of family members of alcoholics who meet regularly to exchange information and to support one another. Being part of an Al-Anon group would provide Sarah with tools to more effectively help her husband stay sober and help her recognize when she unknowingly enables his drinking.

Todd can also set up a time to visit when John is home and has not been drinking. During that visit Sarah, Todd, and other members of the family whom John respects can confront him about his drinking and what it is doing to himself and his family. Limits will need to be set (including the possibility that Sarah will leave unless John gets treatment). Todd should urge John to seek help from his doctor and to enter an alcohol treatment program. Joining an Alcoholics Anonymous (AA) group is an additional option (Corrington, 1989), if John is motivated and willing to stop drinking. For John, quitting is the only option, in light of his other health problems.

John also may have an underlying depression due to his recent health problems and retirement. Therefore, he should be evaluated and treated if he continues to experience depressive symptoms after being sober for several weeks. Antidepressant medications are very effective in late-life depression and may help to replace John's need to self-medicate with alcohol (see the section on mental health specialists, below).

Pastors play an important role in identifying older members of a congregation who may have alcohol problems. Heavy drinkers will seldom acknowledge difficulties with alcohol, so they often slip by unrecognized by the medical system. Since older adults usually do not have job responsibilities, an inability to function at work does not alert others that they have drinking problems. Instead, family members must be relied upon to determine if there is a problem, although they may be too embarrassed to say anything. Knowing a congregation over time and having the trust and respect of members places a pastor in a good position to be able to intervene in difficult situations. Being a friend to an older male alcoholic and providing advice and counsel to affected family members can go a long way toward helping them all get through a challenging time.

In a small church, the pastor may notice that a person does not worship regularly with his or her spouse and can inquire if everything is alright at home. Gentle, persistent support and inquiry will often encourage family members to open up. Some wives actually may be scared to say anything about an alcoholic husband for fear of what he might do. Spouses of alcoholics are at risk for emotional and physical abuse, and a pastor needs to know how to advise them if this occurs. If physical abuse is a concern, action must be taken to move the spouse into a safe setting and possibly to alert legal authorities.

DIAGNOSTIC CRITERIA

As noted in previous cases, there are two types of alcoholism. One is *alcohol abuse* and the other is *alcohol dependence* (APA, 2000). John probably has both. An alcohol abuser may not be alcohol dependent, but an alcohol-dependent person is always an alcohol abuser.

Alcohol abuse is characterized by a pattern of negative, recurrent consequences related to alcohol use. The diagnostic criteria are the same regardless of age. As noted in previous chapters, the diagnosis requires that only one of the following criteria be present during a twelve-month period:

1. Alcohol use results in a failure to fulfill major obligations at home or work.
2. Alcohol is used in situations known to be physically hazardous.
3. Alcohol use is associated with legal problems (e.g., drunk driving, etc.).
4. Alcohol is used despite persistent interpersonal problems resulting from the effects of alcohol.

Alcohol dependence is a pattern of alcohol use that leads to significant impairment or distress as indicated by three or more of the following criteria that occur at any time within the same twelve-month period (APA, 2000):

1. Tolerance, as indicated by either a need for markedly increased amounts of alcohol to achieve intoxication or markedly diminished effect with continued use of the same amount of alcohol.
2. Withdrawal symptoms when alcohol use is decreased and relieved by alcohol intake (two or more of the following symptoms):
   - autonomic hyperactivity such as sweating or rapid heartbeat;
   - tremor;
   - insomnia;
   - nausea or vomiting;
   - transient visual, tactile, or auditory hallucinations or illusions;
   - psychomotor agitation;
   - anxiety; or
   - grand mal seizures.
3. Alcohol is taken in larger amounts or over a longer period than intended.
4. There are unsuccessful efforts to cut down on or control alcohol use.
5. A great deal of time is spent obtaining, using, or recovering from the effects of alcohol.
6. Social, occupational, or recreational activities are reduced because of alcohol use.
7. Alcohol use is continued despite knowledge of persistent or recurrent physical or psychological problems caused or exacerbated by the alcohol.

TREATMENT WITHIN THE FAITH COMMUNITY

There is ample research showing that religious involvement in later life is associated with a decreased risk of both current and lifetime alcohol abuse (Koenig et al., 1994). Religious faith and affiliation are also related to abstinence from alcohol among recovering addicts. In a study of 236 recovering alcoholics or drug addicts, those who reported high levels of religious faith and religious affiliation coped better, had greater resilience to stress, had a more optimistic life orientation, perceived greater social support, and had lower levels of anxiety (Pardini et al., 2000). A study of 156 older adults in either a secular retirement community or a religious one found that those in the religious community had significantly higher life satisfaction, less drinking behaviors, more social interactions, and less death anxiety, compared to those living in the secular retirement community. (Alexander & Duff, 1991)

Encouraging John and Sarah to become more active in the life of the church by participating in ministries, involvement in prayer or Bible study groups, or joining in other religious activity will provide them with cognitive, social, and spiritual resources to help counteract the negative emotions that lead to alcohol abuse or dependence. Such participation will also provide John with a sense of meaning and purpose during his retirement and will enable him to use some of his talents and gifts to serve others as he had done during his working years. Participating in worship and other religious activities together will also strengthen their marital relationship. This will help Sarah by providing social support and involvement outside of the home and will help her be less dependent on what is happening with John if he does not participate.

Bear in mind, however, that both John and Sarah may be embarrassed to reveal their problems to others in the congregation. The faith community plays its most important role in terms of prevention of alcohol abuse and in the maintenance of sobriety, once it has been achieved. Support from the congregation related specifically to the problems that John and Sarah are now having may be limited. Therefore, it is important for Todd to maintain strict confidentiality and not to discuss John and Sarah's problems with anyone in the church without their explicit permission. They may prefer to obtain support outside of the congregation, and Todd can play a role in facilitating that.

If time permits, Todd can accompany John to see a mental health specialist. Todd can offer to go with him to AA meetings (at least at the beginning, until John develops relationships in the group). If John is hospitalized for alcohol detoxification, Todd can visit him in the hospital. Offering such support will help to strengthen Todd's relationship with John so that it can be a resource to help John maintain sobriety after active treatment has ended. If Todd is unable to do these things because of time constraints, then another member of the pastoral care team can fill this role.

TREATMENT BY MENTAL HEALTH SPECIALISTS

Todd will want to keep a list of mental health professionals that he knows and trusts, which can be used to make referrals as they are needed. In this situation, Todd will want to refer John to a mental health specialist who can help him with his current problems. Cognitive-behavioral therapy and treatment with antidepressants may be needed for an underlying depression or problems related to negative thinking or poor self-image. Although John will first need to see his physician (due to his possible need for detoxification and other medical care related to alcohol abuse), he will likely also need treatment by a psychiatrist. Optimally, he or she will have expertise both in the care of older adults (geriatric psychiatry) and in substance-abuse problems. A psychiatrist could help identify and treat an underlying depression or anxiety disorder and enroll John in a substance-abuse treatment program.

John may need counseling to help him deal with issues related to retirement and the changes brought on by his health problems. A counselor can help John identify his gifts and talents, assisting him in finding ways to use those that will give him a renewed sense of meaning and purpose. This will help to counteract the forces that led to his alcohol abuse. Positive and constructive use of John's time will be important to prevent boredom and relapse into drinking. Finally, he will need to develop friendships with persons who do not drink alcohol to replace prior relationships with his drinking buddies. Todd can help to facilitate such friendships by identifying and encouraging men in the congregation with similar interests to spend time with John.

Sarah and John will also need marital counseling to help address the wounds in their relationship that John's drinking has caused. Such pain does not easily heal, even after the drinking stops. While a psychiatrist will have recommendations, Todd may also know of marriage counselors who have a good reputation and who will support John's and Sarah's religious faith and involvement. Todd may choose to do the marital counseling himself, depending on whether he has the time and can be objective in his dealing with both partners.

CONCLUSION

With the help and direction that Todd can provide, the involvement of medical personnel and mental health specialists, and the support of their faith community, John and Sarah have an excellent chance of getting their lives back on track. Retirement can be the best years of life, but only if retirees use their time wisely and invest it in their spiritual growth and in the lives of those who need their gifts, talents, support, and friendship (Koenig, 2002). Pastors can play a significant role in identifying older congregants who are having problems doing that (as indicated by depression, marital problems, or alcohol abuse) and providing them with direction, opportunity, and hope.

HELPFUL BOOKS

Colleran, Carol, and Debra Jay. 2002. *Aging and Addiction: Helping Older Alcohol or Medication Dependency.* Oakland: Springer.

Gurnack, Anne M., Roland Atkinson, and Nancy J. Osgood. 2001. *Treating Alcohol and Drug Abuse in the Elderly.* Oakland: Springer.

Koenig, Harold G. 2003. *Purpose and Power in Retirement: New Opportunities for Meaning and Significance.* Philadelphia: Templeton Foundation Press.

Koenig, Harold G., and Andrew J. Weaver. 1998. *Pastoral Care of Older Adults.* Creative Pastoral Care and Counseling. Minneapolis: Fortress Press.

Weaver, Andrew, and Harold Koenig. 1998. *Reflections on Aging and Spiritual Growth.* Nashville: Abingdon.

6

TWELVE-STEP PROGRAMS

Most individuals who enter treatment for alcohol or drug abuse are referred to twelve-step groups. The oldest and best known of all the twelve-step groups is Alcoholics Anonymous (AA). In addition, most communities also offer chapters of Narcotics Anonymous (NA), Cocaine Anonymous (CA), Gamblers Anonymous (GA), and several other similar groups. All of them are modeled closely on the twelve steps that were developed by the founders of AA.

About 9 percent of U.S. adults say they have attended an AA meeting in their lifetime, and 13 percent have attended a twelve-step program of some type (Room and Greenfield, 1993). These groups can function as caring environments in which members feel safe and secure, offering a natural bridge in the process of reconnecting with the community when addicts are tempted to withdraw and isolate themselves. One of the primary strengths of groups like AA is that they connect persons with others who have struggled with and overcome the same problems that they have.

Twelve-step groups are wholly composed of recovering individuals; no professional leadership is permitted. Recovering persons with long periods of sobriety lead the groups, but any drug or alcohol abusing individuals with a "sincere desire" to recover are welcome to attend. Membership in twelve-step groups is free, although donations are encouraged. Meetings are widespread and frequent, occurring many times a day in most towns and cities.

Twelve-step group formats vary. At speaker meetings, AA members describe their experiences with alcohol, how they came to AA, and how their lives have changed as a result. This is followed by a group discussion on AA recovery and drinking-related problems. Reading meetings that illustrate the twelve steps are also popular. As the word *anonymous* implies, these groups are resolute about keeping their members' identities and what they say anonymous. The rule is "What is said in the rooms, stays in the rooms."

Below are the twelve steps in their original form (Alcoholics Anonymous, 2002). The steps are sometimes summarized as

"Trust God, Clean House, and Help Others." AA makes it clear that the end result of following the steps is finding God as God is understood by the member and establishing a relationship with God. Groups that are focused on other addictions modify the steps somewhat, but retain their essential meanings. The ideal of a twelve-step group is that its members grow to believe and then live each of the twelve steps, which are designed to help an alcoholic achieve a spiritual and psychological state conducive to lasting sobriety. Many AA members believe finding God through the application of the steps has freed them from the urge to drink alcohol.

THE TWELVE STEPS

1. We admitted we were powerless over alcohol in that our lives had become unmanageable.
2. Came to believe that a Power greater than ourselves could restore us to sanity.
3. Made a decision to turn our will and our lives over to the care of God as we understood [God].
4. Made a searching and fearless moral inventory of ourselves.
5. Admitted to God, to ourselves, and to another human being the exact nature of our wrongs.
6. Were entirely ready to have God remove all of these defects of character.
7. Humbly asked [God] to remove our shortcomings.
8. Made a list of all persons we had harmed and became willing to make amends to them all.
9. Made direct amends to such people wherever possible except when doing so would injure them or others.
10. Continued to take moral inventory and when we were wrong promptly admitted it.
11. Sought through prayer and meditation to improve our conscious contact with God as we understood [God], praying only for knowledge of [God's] will for us and the power to carry that out.
12. Having had a spiritual awakening as a result of these steps, we tried to carry this message to alcoholics, and to practice these principles in all our affairs.

The steps are based on principles of surrendering to a Higher Power, asking for forgiveness, and making efforts to make amends for wrongdoing. The founders of AA were Christians, and the message of their twelve steps is steeped in Christian concepts of repentance, redemption, and reconciliation. The twelve steps require surrender to a Power higher and greater than one's self. AA offers for many a meaningful and valuable method to remain drug and alcohol free, based upon spiritual concepts.

Twelve-step participants are helped in learning and living the steps by a sponsor, who is a same-sex recovering person with a history of sobriety. New members to a twelve-step group are strongly encouraged to find a sponsor as soon as possible, since the one-on-one relationship that the sponsor provides is essential to the "working of the steps." To acquire a sponsor, new members must ask someone in the group to be their sponsor. Sponsors encourage their members to contact them while they are craving but before they act on those cravings, so that the sponsor can help the member avoid a relapse. Sponsors also often give their members twelve-step homework and provide guidance about when it is the right time to move to the next step.

Scientific studies show that twelve-step programs have a positive role for many who are in treatment for alcohol addiction. In research conducted by the U.S. Department of Veterans Affairs, patients with alcohol and/or drug use issues who regularly attended twelve-step meetings were doing better after one year than patients who were not involved or were less involved in self-help groups (Moos et al., 2001). The more individuals participated in twelve-step self-help groups in the first year after mental health treatment, the more likely they were to be in remission after five years (Ritsher et al., 2002). Researchers at UCLA found that those who are involved in both AA and professional mental health counseling experience better results than do those who receive only professional treatment (Fiorentine and Hillhouse, 2000).

Research has also found that those who regularly attend AA have increased involvement in faith practices, which leads to sustained recovery over time. This is a particularly important finding when one considers that the AA dropout rate is high (Tonigan, 2007).

HELPFUL BOOKS

Alcoholics Anonymous. 2002. *Big Book of Alcoholics Anonymous.* 4th ed. New York: Alcoholics Anonymous World Services.

Anonymous. 1994. *A Day at a Time: Daily Reflections for Recovering People.* Minneapolis: Hazelden.

Anonymous. 1996. *Twenty-Four Hours A Day.* Minneapolis: Hazelden.

Anonymous. 2002. *Living Sober.* Minneapolis: Hazelden.

Anonymous. 2002. *Twelve Steps and Twelve Traditions.* 38th print ed. Minneapolis: Hazelden.

Kettelhack, Guy. 1998. *First Year Sobriety: When All That Changes Is Everything.* Minneapolis: Hazelden.

7

MAKING AN
EFFECTIVE REFERRAL

An individual in the United States is more likely to seek a clergyperson for help with a serious mental health difficulty, such as alcohol abuse or dependency, than to go to a psychologist or psychiatrist. Unfortunately, most of those who need specialized care do not subsequently contact a mental health professional after being counseled by a pastor (Hohmann and Larson, 1993).

It is essential for the responsible practice of ministry that clergy and other religious professionals be prepared to recognize persons with alcohol-related problems and make effective referrals (Hatchett et al., 2007). A central task of pastors within a mental health network is to identify the needs of individuals who seek their assistance and to connect them to a larger circle of specialized helpers (Grauf-Grounds and Backton, 2007). This chapter makes several suggestions as to how clergy can increase their effectiveness at making referrals to mental health specialists who work with alcohol-related issues.

DEVELOP WORKING RELATIONSHIPS WITH
MENTAL HEALTH PROFESSIONALS

It is important to develop a working relationship with at least one, preferably several, mental health professionals who have a comprehensive knowledge of the services available in your community for alcohol related problems and are willing to work with you as a colleague. Other clergy in the community who have a reputation for being psychologically minded are often an excellent resource when developing your mental health resources network. Inquire as to which mental health professionals have been most helpful and make a list of contacts with whom to follow up.

There are a range of mental health professionals who can evaluate and treat alcohol and related disorders, including psychologists, psychiatrists, clinical social workers, marriage and family therapists, psychiatric nurses, pastoral counselors, and several other types of licensed counselors and therapists.

- *Psychologists* are mental health professionals with a research degree (Ph.D. or Psy.D.) who are trained to provide evaluation, assessment, testing, and treatment of mental disorders with individuals and families. After earning their degree, they must complete two or more years of additional training before they can be licensed for independent practice.
- *Psychiatrists* are physicians with special training in mental health issues who can prescribe medications. After earning a medical degree (M.D.), they must complete four years of residency training at a teaching hospital.
- *Social workers* with a graduate degree (M.S.W.) are professionally trained in coordinating access to available community services, and some with special training have clinical practices. In order to offer psychotherapy, clinical social workers must be licensed by their state. Once licensed, they are designated as licensed clinical social worker (L.C.S.W.) or licensed independent clinical social workers (L.I.C.S.W).
- *Marriage and family therapists* usually have earned at least a master's degree training them to work with marital and family problems. After earning their degree, most are required to complete two or more years of additional training under supervision before they can be licensed for independent practice.
- *Psychiatric nurses* are licensed registered nurses (R.N.) who have additional training in mental health. They work with individuals, families, or communities to evaluate mental health needs and assist other mental health professionals in treatment and referral.
- *Advanced practice registered nurses* (A.P.R.N.) have a master's degree in psychiatric-mental health nursing. There are two types of A.P.R.N.s: clinical nurse specialists and nurse practitioners. In general, they can diagnose and treat mental illnesses, and in many states they are authorized to prescribe medications. They also may be qualified to practice independently, without the supervision of a doctor. Additionally, there are several thousand parish-based nurses in the United

States—a movement that is growing rapidly (Patterson, 2003).

- *Pastoral counselors* who have seminary training (M.Div.) and frequently are licensed to practice in one of the other mental health disciplines are the mental health specialists with whom clergy most often work. Their specialty integrates theological and psychological training that makes them particularly equipped to understand and assist clergy colleagues.

Interview a mental health professional in person or by telephone before you refer someone who trusts you to make an educated referral. Keep a record of available providers to whom you can refer in an emergency. Ask the specialists direct questions to assess their skill level, expertise, and fee schedule. Inquire in detail about their experience, training, and education. For example:

- What license do they have and how many years have they practiced? Credentials can also be checked by contacting state licensing boards.
- What are their office hours, fees, length of sessions? Which insurance providers do they work with? Do they accept Medicare or Medicaid?
- What sorts of issues have they worked with in the past? Mental health providers often specialize in specific disorders or age groups.
- Have they worked with individuals and families suffering from alcoholism?
- How do they develop treatment plans for various substance-abuse disorders and crisis situations?
- How easily can they be located in an emergency?
- Are they willing to do some *pro bono* or low-fee work?

It is important to create a list of professional and community resources before you are faced with a mental health emergency. Equip yourself with such knowledge as: the location of the nearest hospital emergency room, in case a person becomes psychotic, suicidal, or violent; the location of the closest outpatient mental health center; which social services are available; and how they can be accessed in an emergency.

PREPARING A PERSON FOR REFERRAL

Persuading someone to see a mental health professional has little value if the individual is not prepared to accept help. A clergyperson needs to foster an open and trusting relationship and encourage the person to share his or her feelings about the proposed referral. Acknowledging an individual's doubts, fears, and frustrations about having problems that require mental health care may be needed. Some people think that only those with severe mental health problems need therapy, so they may experience your referral as judgmental and condemning. Reassure the person that therapists work with those who have concerns that are both small and large. Problems need not reach crisis proportions for individuals to benefit from professional help. In fact, it is much easier to work on issues if they are addressed before they reach crisis level. It is often useful to make the point that it takes genuine courage to face one's difficulties and limitations. Normalizing the process of seeking help may be especially important when referring those whose cultures may not have similar views of psychological counseling.

A pastor should make clear why a referral is being made and emphasize that he or she will continue to provide spiritual support and guidance. It is important to affirm that the congregation will be supportive as an individual and his or her family work through emerging issues. A referral is not a rejection. It assists a person in finding additional sources of information and necessary specialized care. It is important for a religious leader to acknowledge when one does not have the expertise required to assist someone in dealing with his or her issues, which is precisely why a referral is often required. Encourage the person to report back on the helpfulness, or lack of it, when a referral is made. This can be valuable in evaluating a mental health professional, agency, or support group.

CONTINUING EDUCATION IS IMPORTANT

Unlike growth in other areas of pastoral ministry (such as administration, preaching, teaching), clergy report that no matter how long they serve, they believe that their counseling skills do not improve without continuing education (Orthner, 1986). Research has demonstrated that training clergy in diagnostic skills enhances their ability as pastoral counselors, as well as their effectiveness in making referrals (Clemens et al., 1978). Pastors must understand that a timely referral is an act of responsible pastoral care. Clergy can serve most effectively in the mental health network as skilled facilitators who identify the needs of persons and then connect them to a larger circle of specialized helpers (Grauf-Grounds and Backton, 2007).

SELF-CARE IS A MUST

Clergy have numerous responsibilities that place extensive requirements on their time and energy, requiring good self-care practices to keep them emotionally healthy and effective. There are few occasions when pastors are not "on call," and they often must deal with persons who are severely troubled. In part because of time demands and financial pressures, the burnout syndrome has become increasingly associated with pastoral work (Jones, 2001). It is important, given the high emotional demands on clergy offering pastoral care and counseling, that they develop sound self-care skills. Here are some suggestions:

- Spend time with others. Be willing to ask for support and assistance from your family, friends, colleagues, or community resources. Join or create support groups.
- Talk about how you feel. Helping professionals know that human feelings are powerful. Venting is cathartic—it is a helpful process by which people use words and nonverbal communication to let go of distressing emotions.
- Take time to grieve and cry, if needed. In the long run, to function well you must let painful feelings out instead of pushing them away or hiding them.
- Treatment by a mental health professional who is open to a person of faith can be of an important act of self-care. Clergy in emotional distress are limited in their ability to help those in need of assistance.
- Set small goals to tackle big problems. Approach one thing at a time instead of trying to do everything at once. If you are attempting to do too much, eliminate or delay the things that are not absolutely necessary.

- Eat healthfully and take time to walk, stretch, exercise, and relax, even if just for a few minutes at a time. Make sure you get enough rest. You may need more sleep than usual when you are under high stress.
- Do something that feels good, like taking a warm bath, sitting in the sun, or spending time with a pet. Celebrate your sense of humor.

HELPFUL ORGANIZATIONS

Al-Anon Family Groups; 1600 Corporate Landing Parkway, Virginia Beach, VA 23454-5617; (888) 425-2666; www.al-anon. alateen.org. Al-Anon is an international organization with 32,000+ groups. It was founded in 1951 as a fellowship of men, women, children, and adult children whose lives have been affected by the compulsive drinking of a family member or friend. The program is based on the twelve steps of Alcoholics Anonymous. Literature is available in twenty-nine languages.

Alcoholics Anonymous World Services; General Service Office, P.O. Box 459, New York, NY 10163; (212) 870-3400; www. aa.org. AA is a worldwide fellowship of women and men. The only requirement for membership is a desire to stop drinking alcohol. Members observe personal anonymity at the public level, emphasizing AA principles rather than personalities. For more information, check the local phone directory or newspaper.

American Association for Marriage and Family Therapy; 112 South Alfred St., Alexandria, VA 22314-3061; (703) 838-9808; www. aamft.org. AAMFT offers continuing education programs for those who work with families.

American Association of Pastoral Counselors; 9504A Lee Highway, Fairfax, VA 22031-2303; (703) 385-6967; www.aapc.org. AAPC provides information on qualified pastoral counselors and church related counseling centers.

American Psychiatric Association; 1000 Wilson Boulevard, Suite 1825, Arlington, VA 22209-3901; (888) 357-7924; www.psych. org.

American Psychological Association; 750 First Street NE, Washington, DC 20002-4242; (800) 374-2721; www.apa.org.

Association for Clinical Pastoral Education; 1549 Clairmont Road, Suite 103, Decatur, GA 30033; (404) 320-1472; www.acpe.edu. ACPE is an interfaith organization that fosters training in pastoral care and counseling through programs of clinical pastoral education.

Association of Professional Chaplains; 1701 East Woodfield Road, Suite 400, Schaumburg, IL 60173; (847) 240-1014; www.professionalchaplains.org. An interfaith organization of Jewish, Protestant, and Roman Catholic clergy.

Canadian Association for Pastoral Practice and Education; 660 Francklyn Street, Halifax, Nova Scotia B3H 385, Canada; (866) 442-2773; www.cappe.org.

Interfaith Health Program, Rollins School of Public Health, Emory University, 1256 Briarcliff Road, NE, Building A, Suite 107, Atlanta, GA 30306; (404) 727-5246; www.ihpnet.org.

International Parish Nurse Resource Center; 475 East Lockwood Avenue, St. Louis, MO 63119; (314) 918-2559; www.parish nurses.org.

National Association of Social Workers; 750 First Street NE, Suite 700, Washington, DC 20002-4241; (202) 408-8600; www.socialworkers.org.

National Organization for Continuing Education of Roman Catholic Clergy; 333 North Michigan Avenue, Suite 1205, Chicago, IL 60601; (312) 781-9450; www.nocercc.org.

Samaritan Institute; 2696 South Colorado, Suite 380, Denver, CO 80222; (303) 691-0144; www.samaritaninstitute.org. Helps communities develop interfaith counseling centers.

Stephen Ministries; 2045 Innerbelt Business Center Drive, St. Louis, MO 63114; (314) 428-2600; www.stephenministries.org. Offers training in counseling skills for local church members for peer ministry.

HELPFUL BOOKS

Jones, Kirk Byron. 2001. *Rest in the Storm: Self-Care Strategies for Clergy and Other Caregivers.* Valley Forge, Pa.: Judson.

Jones, Kirk Byron. 2007. *Holy Play: The Joyful Adventure of Unleashing Your Divine Purpose.* New York: Jossey-Bass.

McBride, J. Lebron. 2005. *Living Faithfully with Disappointment in the Church.* Binghamton, N.Y.: Haworth.

Miller, William R., and Kathleen A. Jackson. 1995. *Practical Psychology for Pastors*. Englewood Cliffs, N.J.: Prentice-Hall.

Nouwen, Henri J. M. 1979. *The Wounded Healer*. New York: Doubleday.

Nouwen, Henri J. M. 1982. *The Way of the Heart*. New York: Ballantine.

Oswald, Roy M. 1991. *Clergy Self-Care: Finding a Balance for Effective Ministry*. Bethesda, Md.: Alban Institute.

Pappas, Anthony G. 1995. *Pastoral Stress*. Bethesda, Md.: Alban Institute.

Randall, Robert L., and James B. Nelson. 1998. *Walking Through the Valley: Understanding and Emerging from Clergy Depression*. Nashville: Abingdon.

Weidner, Hal. 2006. *Grief, Loss, and Death: The Shadow Side of Ministry*. Binghamton, N.Y.: Haworth.

RESOURCES

There are innumerable international, national, state, and local organizations that help people struggling with addictive behaviors, as well as countless groups focused on the related issues of family members, co-workers, and other associated. Those cited here are representative, but by no means exhaustive of the resources available. The addresses, phone numbers, and Web sites are all current as of April 2009.

ALCOHOLISM

Al-Anon Family Groups; 1600 Corporate Landing Parkway, Virginia Beach, VA 23454-5617; (888) 4AL-ANON; www.al-anon.alateen.org. An international organization with 32,000 + groups. It was founded in 1951 as a fellowship of men, women, children, and adult children whose lives have been affected by the compulsive drinking of a family member or friend. The program is based on the twelve steps of AA. Literature available in twenty-nine languages.

Alcoholics Anonymous World Services; General Service Office, P.O. Box 459, Grand Central Station, New York, NY 10163; (212) 870-3400; www.alcoholics-anonymous.org. A worldwide fellowship of women and men. The only requirement for membership is a desire to stop drinking. Members observe personal anonymity at the public level, emphasizing AA principles rather than personalities. For more information, check the local phone directory or newspaper.

Alcoholics Victorious; 4501 Troost Street, Kansas City, MO 64110-4127; (816) 561-0567; www.alcoholicsvictorious.org. A Christian-oriented twelve-step support group for recovering alcoholics. Information, referrals, literature, phone support, conferences, support group meetings, and a newsletter are available.

American Council for Drug Education; 164 West 74th Street, New York, NY 10023; (800) 488-DRUG; www.acde.org.

American Society of Addiction Medicine (ASAM); 4601 N. Park Avenue, Upper Arcade, Suite 101, Chevy Chase, MD 20815; (301) 656-3920; www.asam.org. A medical society dedicated to educating physicians and improving the treatment of individuals suffering from alcoholism and other addictions.

Calix Society; 3881 Highland Ave., Suite 201, White Bear Lake, MN 55110; (800) 398-0524; www.calixsociety.org. An international fellowship of Roman Catholic alcoholics maintaining their sobriety through Alcoholics Anonymous. It is concerned with total abstinence, spiritual development, and sanctification of the whole personality of each member.

Centers for Disease Control and Prevention; Alcohol and Public Health, 4770 Buford Hwy, NE, Mailstop K-67, Atlanta, GA 30341-3717; (800) 662-HELP; www.cdc.gov/alcohol/index .htm. An agency of the U.S. Department of Health and Human Services; provides fact and statistics related to alcohol consumption, binge drinking, heavy drinking, alcohol dependence, and underage drinking. Their Web site provides links to other related Web sites.

Dual Recovery Anonymous; P.O. Box 8107, Prairie Village, KS 66208; (877) 883-2332; draonline.org. An international twelve-step self-help program for individuals who experience a dual disorder of both chemical dependency and a psychiatric illness. It provides literature, a newsletter, and assistance in starting local groups.

Hazelden Foundation; CO3, P.O. Box 11, Center City, MN 55012-0011; (800) 257-7810; www.hazelden.org.

Jewish Alcoholics, Chemically Dependent Persons, and Significant Others; 120 West 57th Street, New York, NY 10019; (212) 397-4197; www.jacsweb.org.

Mothers Against Drunk Driving (MADD); 511 E. John Carpenter Freeway, Suite 700, Irving, TX 75062; (800) GET-MADD; www.madd.org. An educational and advocacy organization with four hundred chapters. It is devoted to heightening awareness of the dangers of impaired driving.

National Center on Addiction and Substance Abuse at Columbia University; 633 Third Avenue, 19th Floor, New York, NY 10017-6706; (212) 841-5200; www.casacolumbia.org.

National Clearinghouse for Alcohol and Drug Information (NCADI); P.O. Box 2345, Rockville, MD 20847-2345; (800)

729-6686; TDD: (800) 487-4899; ncadi.samhsa.gov. Provides free materials about many aspects of alcohol and drug abuse treatment and prevention. Several of these publications are designed for the faith community.

National Council on Alcoholism and Drug Dependence; 244 East 58th Street, 4th floor, New York, NY 10022; (212) 269-7797; www.ncadd.org. A nonprofit organization that offers information and referral services through two hundred state and local affiliates. It provides preventive educational programs for community organizations such as churches and temples. Persons seeking assistance can contact their area affiliate or call a national toll-free help line: (800) 622-2255.

National Families in Action; 2957 Clairmont Road, N.E., Suite 150, Atlanta, GA 30329; (404) 248-9676; www.nationalfamilies .org.

National Institute on Alcohol Abuse and Alcoholism; 5635 Fishers Lane, MSC 9304, Bethesda, MD 20892-9304; (301) 443-3860; www.niaaa.nih.gov. Supports and conducts research on the causes, consequences, treatment, and prevention of alcoholism and alcohol-related problems.

Overcomers Outreach; 12828 Acheson Dr., Whittier, CA 90601; (800) 310-3001; www.overcomersoutreach.org. A Christian-oriented twelve-step support group found in most states.

Recovered Alcoholic Clergy Association; www.racapecusa.org. A national network for clergy of the Episcopal Church supporting one another in their recovery from alcoholism. Also provides assistance to clergy (and their families) who are in trouble with drinking issues.

SMART Recovery; 7537 Mentor Avenue, Suite 306, Mentor, OH 44060; (866) 951-5357; www.smartrecovery.org. A national network of self-help groups for individuals wanting to gain their independence from addictive and compulsive behaviors. It is an abstinence program based on cognitive-behavioral principles, especially those of rational-emotive-behavior therapy. It provides information and referrals, literature and assistance in starting local chapters.

The Salvation Army; 615 Slater Lane, P.O. Box 269, Alexandria, VA 22313; (703) 684-5528; www.salvationarmyusa.org.

Women For Sobriety, P.O. Box 618, Quakertown, PA 18951-0618; (215) 536-8026; www.womenforsobriety.org. A nonprofit organization dedicated to helping women overcome alcoholism and other addictions. The group offers monthly newsletter, information and referrals, phone support, group meetings, conferences and group development guidelines.

DEPRESSION AND GRIEF

American Association of Pastoral Counselors; 9504A Lee Highway, Fairfax, VA 22031-2303; (703) 385-6967; www.aapc.org. Provides information on qualified pastoral counselors and church related counseling centers.

American Foundation for Suicide Prevention; 120 Wall Street, 22nd Floor, New York, NY 10005; (888) 333-2377. Provides state-by-state directories of survivor support groups for families and friends of a suicide.

American Psychiatric Association; 1000 Wilson Boulevard, Suite 1825, Arlington, VA 22209-3901; (888) 357-7924; www.psych.org.

American Psychological Association; 750 First Street NE, Washington, DC 20002-4242; (800) 374-2721; www.apa.org.

Boys Town National Hotline; 14100 Crawford Street, Boys Town, NE 68010; (800) 448-3000; www.girlsandboystown.org. Provides short-term counseling and referrals to local resources, including U.S. territories and Canada. Counsels on parent-child conflicts, suicide, depression, pregnancy, runaways, and abuse. Spanish-speaking operators are available. Operates twenty-four hours a day.

Centering Corporation; 7230 Maple Street, Omaha, NE, 68134; (866) 218-0101; www.centeringcorp.com. A nonprofit organization founded in 1977 and dedicated to providing education and resources for the bereaved; on-line store offers over three hundred books, *Grief Digest* magazine, and other related resources.

Centre for Suicide Prevention; Suite 320, 1202 Centre St. S.E., Calgary, Alberta, Canada T2G 5A5; (403) 245-3900; www.suicideinfo.ca. Provides information on suicide education and a suicide-prevention training program.

The Compassionate Friends (TCF); P.O. Box 3696, Oak Brook, IN 60522-3696; (877) 969-0010; www.compassionatefriends.org. A nonprofit, self-help support organization for bereaved parents, grandparents, and siblings; provides chapter locator and links to chapter Web sites, brochures, grief resources, national magazine, and sibling resources.

National Depressive and Manic-Depressive Association; 730 N. Franklin Street, Suite 501, Chicago, IL 60654-7225; (800) 826-3632; www.ndmda.org.

National Suicide Hotline; (800) SUICIDE (784-2433).

National Youth Crisis Hotline; (800) 448-4663. Provides counseling and referrals to local counseling services. Responds to youth dealing with pregnancy, molestation, suicide, and child abuse. Operates twenty-four hours a day.

Rainbows; 2100 Golf Road, Suite 370, Rolling Meadows, IL 60008; (847) 952-1700; www.rainbows.org. An international organization with 6,300 affiliated groups. Founded in 1983, Rainbows establishes peer support groups in churches, schools, and social agencies for children and adults who are grieving a divorce, death, or other painful change in their family. The groups are led by trained adults, and referrals are provided.

Suicide Awareness Voices of Education (SAVE); 8120 Penn Avenue S., Suite 470, Bloomington, MN 55431; (952) 946-7998; www.save.org. An organization dedicated to educating the public about suicide prevention.

Survivors Helping Survivors; St. Luke's Medical Center, 2900 West Oklahoma Avenue, Milwaukee, WI 53215; (414) 219-7067. Gives support to those who have lost loved ones to suicide.

Stephen Ministries; 2045 Innerbelt Business Center Drive, St. Louis, MO 63114-5765; (314) 428-2600; www.stephen ministries.org. Offers training in counseling skills for local church members for peer ministry.

GAMBLING

California Council on Problem Gambling; 800 South Harbor Boulevard, Suite 255, Anaheim, CA 92805; (800) 522-4700; www.calproblemgambling.org. A statewide organization made up of individuals from clinical, academic, and research disciplines, as well as recovering compulsive gamblers and their families.

Chinese Community Problem Gambling Project; NICOS Chinese Health Coalition, 1208 Mason Street, San Francisco, CA 94108; (415) 788-6426; www.nicoschc.com. Provides a problem gambling self-assessment in both Chinese and English, as well as articles in both languages.

Gam-Anon; P.O. Box 157, Whitestone, NY 11357; (718) 352-1671; www.gam-anon.org, An international organization with 380 groups, founded in 1960. It is a fellowship of women and men who are family members and friends of compulsive gamblers affected by the gambling problem. The aim of the program is to rebuild lives and give aid to gamblers and their families. There are Gam-a-teen groups for teens. Group guidelines and other literature are available.

Gamblers Anonymous (GA); P.O. Box 17173, Los Angeles, CA 90017; (213) 386-8789; www.gamblersanonymous.org. An international organization founded in 1957, with 1,200 chapters. It is a fellowship of men and women who share experiences, strength, and hope with each other to recover from compulsive gambling, following a twelve-step program. GA publishes a monthly bulletin for members.

Institute for Research on Pathological Gambling and Related Disorders; Division on Addictions, Cambridge Health Alliance, Harvard Medical School, 101 Station Landing, 2nd Floor, Medford, MA 02155; (781) 306-8600; www.divisionon addictions.org/institute. Established in 2000 as a program of Harvard Medical School's Division on Addictions. Its mission is to alleviate the individual, social, medical, and economic burdens caused by pathological gambling through support of rigorous scientific research.

Know the Odds; P.O. Box 3079, Auburn, Victoria, Australia 3123; 0417.107.440; www.knowodds.org. Has educational materials for schools and colleges to help prevent the harmful effects of problem gambling.

National Center for Responsible Gambling; 1299 Pennsylvania Avenue NW, Suite 1175, Washington, DC 20004; (202) 552-2689; www.ncrg.org. Founded in 1996 to help individuals and families affected by gambling disorders. It was the first national organization exclusively devoted to funding scientific research on pathological gambling.

Stop Predatory Gambling Foundation; 100 Maryland Avenue NE, Room 311, Washington, DC 20002; (202) 567-6996; www.ncalg .org. Offers information on the adverse personal, social, economic, and public health effects of gambling. The founder of the organization is a United Methodist minister, Thomas Grey.

National Council on Problem Gambling; 730 11th Street NW, Suite 601, Washington, DC 20001; (800) 522-4700; www. ncpgambling.org. A nonprofit health agency whose mission is to provide information about compulsive gambling and to promote the development of services for those suffering from pathological gambling.

North American Training Institute; 314 West Superior Street, Suite 508, Duluth, MN 55802; (888) 989-9234; www.nati.org. A division of the Minnesota Council on Compulsive Gambling. It has training programs for senior citizens and adolescents including *Wanna Bet* magazine for kids concerned about gambling.

Overcomers Outreach; 12828 Acheson Drive, Whittier, CA 90601; (800) 310-3001; www.overcomersoutreach.org. A Christian-oriented twelve-step program with one thousand support groups for teens with any type of compulsive behavior, including gambling.

POST-TRAUMATIC STRESS DISORDER

American Association of Pastoral Counselors; 9504A Lee Highway, Fairfax, VA 22031-2303; (703) 385-6967; www.aapc.org. Provides information on qualified pastoral counselors and church-related counseling centers.

American Counseling Association; 5999 Stevenson Avenue, Alexandria, VA 22304; (800) 347-6647; www.counseling.org.

American Psychiatric Association; 1000 Wilson Boulevard, Suite 1825, Arlington, VA 22209-3901; (888) 357-7924; www.psych .org.

American Psychological Association; 750 First Street NE, Washington, DC 20002-4242; (800) 374-2721; www.apa.org.

Anxiety Disorders Association of America; 8730 Georgia Avenue, Suite 600, Silver Spring, MD 20910; (240) 485-1001; www.adaa.org.

Gift From Within; 16 Cobb Hill Road, Camden, ME 04843; (207) 236-8858; www.giftfromwithin.org. A nonprofit organization dedicated to helping those who suffer from PTSD. It maintains a roster of trauma survivors who participate in a national network for peer support.

International Society for Traumatic Stress Studies; 111 Deer Lake Road, Suite 100, Deerfield, IL 60015; (847) 480-9028; www.istss.org.

National Center for Post-Traumatic Stress Disorder; VA Medical Center, 215 North Main Street, White River Junction, VT 05009; (802) 296-6300; www.ncptsd.org. Provides information for families, employers, and communities to help support returning veterans in their transition from military to civilian life. Resources and readings are provided, as well as information on preparing for returning veterans, career transition tools, support networks, and more.

Post Traumatic Stress Disorder Alliance; www.ptsdalliance.org. A multidisciplinary group that provides educational resources to health care professionals and those diagnosed with PTSD.

Sidran Institute; 200 East Joppa Road, Suite 207, Baltimore, MD 21286-3107; (410) 825-8888; www.sidran.org. Focuses on education, advocacy, and research related to the early recognition and treatment of traumatic stress disorders.

U.S. Department of Veteran Affairs (VA); www.va.gov. This website is a resource that provides information on VA programs, veteran's benefits, and VA facilities worldwide. The VA is the parent organization of the National Center for PTSD.

GLOSSARY

Abstinence: To refrain from the usage of alcohol.

Addiction: A state of dependence based on tolerance (a need for increased amounts of alcohol for intoxication to occur or lessened effect with the same amount of substance), withdrawal symptoms or using alcohol to avoid withdrawal symptoms, an inability to control use, and/or alcohol use that has a negative effect on one's social, occupational, or recreational life or on one's physical or psychological health.

Al-Anon: An organization dedicated to helping the families and friends of alcoholics, using the structure of a support group and the twelve-step program.

Alcohol: The intoxicating chemical in beverages such as beer, wine, and distilled liquor. Alcohol is a colorless, volatile liquid also called ethanol or ethyl alcohol. It is a central nervous system depressant.

Alcohol abuse: The continued use of alcohol, despite the development of social, legal, or health problems.

Alcoholics Anonymous (AA): The organization that developed the twelve-step approach to recovery from alcohol addiction (alcoholism). Many groups have adopted this method to help people recover from addiction to other drugs, such as Narcotics Anonymous (NA) and Cocaine Anonymous (CA).

Alcoholism: A chronic disease characterized by a strong craving for alcohol, a constant or periodic reliance on the use of alcohol despite adverse consequences, the inability to limit drinking, physical illness when drinking is stopped, and the need for increasing amounts of alcohol to feel its effects.

Big Book: The nickname for the volume *Alcoholics Anonymous*, the "textbook" of the twelve-step recovery program of the same name, first published in 1939.

Binge drinking: A pattern of heavy drinking that occurs during a period of time set aside for drinking. It has been described as 5/4 drinking: five or more drinks in a row on a single occasion for a man or four or more drinks for a woman.

Blackout: A period of memory loss for which there is no recall of activities as a result of alcohol consumption.

Blood alcohol concentration: The amount of alcohol in the blood expressed as a percent (grams of ethanol per 100 milliliters of blood).

Chronic: Long-term; refers to diseases, habits, or conditions that last a long time, recur, or are difficult to cure.

Cirrhosis: Hardening of connective tissue in the liver, which is often the result of alcoholism.

Cognitive: Having to do with the ability to think or reason; sometimes used to describe the memory process; the operation of the mind as distinct from emotions.

Cognitive-behavior therapy: A form of psychological treatment that focuses on directly modifying both a person's thought process and behavior.

Compulsion: An intrusive, repetitive, and unwanted urge to perform an act that is counter to a person's usual conduct.

Coping: The process of using personal, spiritual, and/or social resources to manage stress.

Craving: A powerful, often uncontrollable, desire for alcohol.

Crisis intervention: Emergency assistance that focuses on providing guidance and support to help mobilize the resources needed to resolve a serious problem.

Delirium tremens (DTs): A serious alcohol-withdrawal syndrome observed in persons who stop drinking alcohol following continuous and heavy consumption. It includes profound confusion, hallucinations, and severe nervous system overactivity, typically beginning between forty-eight and ninety-six hours after the last drink.

Denial: Refusing to admit that a person is addicted or to accept the degree of harm caused by an addiction.

Depression: Emotional disturbance in which a person feels unhappy and often has trouble sleeping, eating, and/or concentrating.

Detoxification: A process of withdrawing a person from alcohol in a safe manner.

Diagnosis: The process of collecting data to identify and evaluate a problem and the conclusion reached as a result of that process.

***Diagnostic and Statistical Manual of Mental Disorders*, Fourth Edition, Text Revision (DSM-IV-TR)**: The official manual of mental health problems developed by the American Psychiatric Association. This reference volume is used by mental health professionals to understand and diagnose psychological problems.

Disorder: A mental health problem that impairs an individual's social, educational, or mental functioning or significantly interferes with her or his quality of life.

Distillation: A process that uses heat to purify or separate a complex substance. Various components of the mixture are collected as gases and condensed to liquids. Liquor is produced through distillation.

Dual diagnosis: A term used to describe patients with mental health disorders and coexisting substance addictions, such as alcoholism.

DUI/DWI: Drunk driving—known as driving under the influence (DUI) or driving while intoxicated (DWI). In some states, it is known as OUI (operating a motor vehicle under the influence).

Dysfunctional: Abnormal or impaired functioning.

Enabling: Any action by one person that intentionally or unintentionally has the effect of facilitating the continuation of another individual's addictive process.

Family therapy: A therapeutic method that involves assessment and treatment by including immediate family members. This model emphasizes the family as a whole, rather than focusing on one person.

Fermentation: A process that converts sugar into alcohol and carbon dioxide. This phenomenon is used to make wine and beer.

Fetal alcohol syndrome: A pattern of mental and physical birth abnormalities found in some children of mothers who drink alcohol during pregnancy.

Impairment: Diminished ability to function normally, such as when alcohol decreases motor function or interferes with thinking.

Intoxication: The condition of being drunk. An abnormal state that is essentially alcohol poisoning. It is characterized by slurred speech and a loss of coordination.

MADD (Mothers Against Drunk Driving): An organization that promotes public awareness about the dangers of drunk driving and works to pass strict drunk-driving laws.

Normalizing: A therapeutic strategy that depathologizes problems in a way that changes a person's perceptions of a situation and defuses the difficulty.

Outpatient treatment: Nonresidential medical treatment where patients live at home, often are employed, and go to a clinic for treatment.

Overdose: The condition that results when too much of a substance is taken, making a person sick or unconscious and sometimes resulting in a serious toxic reaction and death.

Parish nurse: A nurse working from a congregation, promoting all aspects of wellness. Parish nurses train and coordinate volunteers, develop support groups, liaison within the health-care system, refer to community resources, and provide health education.

Physical dependence: When a person requires the regular use of alcohol or another drug in order to function and develops withdrawal symptoms without the substance.

Post-traumatic stress disorder (PTSD): An anxiety disorder in which symptoms develop following psychological trauma. The essential features of PTSD include increased physical arousal, intrusive reexperiencing of the traumatic event, and avoidance.

Predispose: To make susceptible, such as to certain health problems or to alcohol dependency. For example, certain family of origin issues can predispose an individual to develop alcoholism.

Prognosis: A forecast about the outcome of a condition, including an indication of its probable duration and course.

Psychiatrist: A physician who has special training (medical residency in psychiatry) to deal with psychological problems. A psychiatrist can hospitalize patients and may treat with medications, psychotherapy, or both.

Psychological dependence: Mental or emotional feelings of discomfort when alcohol or other drug of choice is not available.

Psychological trauma: An event that is outside the range of usual human experience, which is so distressing as to cause emotional difficulties by overwhelming a person's ability to cope.

Psychologist: A mental health professional with an advanced degree (Ph.D. or Psy.D.) who is trained to use a variety of treatment methods, including individual and group therapy and family systems. She or he is also trained to do psychological testing.

Psychopharmacology: The management of mental illness using medication.

Psychosis: A severe mental condition that involves hallucinations, delusions, and/or paranoia.

Psychosomatic: A physical disorder of the body caused or aggravated by emotional stress.

Psychotherapy: A process in which an individual seeks to resolve problems or achieve psychological growth through oral communication with a mental health professional.

Reframing: Putting a situation or behavior into a new, more positive perspective, thus changing the context in which it is understood.

Regression: A process in which a person exhibits behavior that is more appropriate to an earlier stage of development.

Rehabilitation: Restoration to good health or a useful life, through support, therapy, and/or education. The process of quitting drinking and learning how to remain abstinent.

Relapse: The return to uncontrolled drinking after a period of abstinence or moderate use.

Self-help groups: Therapeutic groups that function without the leadership of health professionals.

Sobriety: The condition of refraining from drinking alcohol.

Social worker (M.S.W.): A mental health professional who is trained to understand and emphasize the effect of environmental factors on mental problems. He or she often assists individuals and their families in locating and accessing available community services.

Sponsor: In twelve-step support groups, a sponsor is usually a longtime member, chosen by a newcomer to help teach the program of recovery and the twelve steps. A sponsor is a volunteer who has worked the steps him- or herself.

Stress: Tension resulting from a person's response to his or her environment.

Stupor: A state of impaired consciousness accompanied by diminished responsiveness to surroundings.

Substance abuse: Excess, abnormal, or illegal use of drugs or alcohol.

Tolerance: A condition in which increasingly higher doses of alcohol are required to produce the same effect as during prior use.

Trauma: A serious physical or emotional occurrence that causes substantial damage to a person's psychological or physical state, often causing lasting aftereffects (e.g., war, disaster, serious car accident, rape, assault, molestation, sudden death of a significant other, etc.).

Withdrawal: Symptoms that occur after chronic use of alcohol is reduced or stopped, such as severe alcohol cravings and physical and psychological problems.

Zero-tolerance laws: Laws that exist in all fifty states and the District of Columbia making it illegal for anyone under the age of twenty-one to drive a car after drinking any alcohol.

BIBLIOGRAPHY

Adams, W. L. 1998. Late life outcomes: Health services use and the clinical encounter. In Gomberg, E. S. L., Hegedus, A. M., and Zucker, R. A., *Alcohol Problems and Aging*. NIAAA Research Monograph No. 33. NIH Pub. No. 98-4163. Bethesda, Md.: NIAAA.

Alcoholics Anonymous. 2002. *Big Book of Alcoholics Anonymous*. 4th ed. New York: Alcoholics Anonymous World Services.

American Psychiatric Association (APA). 2000. *Diagnostic and Statistical Manual of Mental Disorders*. 4th ed., text revision. Washington, D.C.: American Psychiatric Association.

Atkinson, R. M., Tolson, R. L., and Turner, J. A. 1990. Late versus early onset problem drinking in older men. *Alcohol Clinical and Experimental Research* 14, no. 4:574–79.

Bahr, S. J., Hawk, R. D., and Wang, G. 1993. Family and religious influences on adolescent substance abuse. *Youth and Society*, 24, no. 4: 443–65.

Beckham, J. C, Feldman, M. E., and Kirby, A. C. 1998. Atrocities exposure in Vietnam combat veterans with chronic post-traumatic stress disorder: Relationship to combat exposure, symptom severity, guilt, and interpersonal violence. *Journal of Trauma Stress* 11, no. 4:777–85.

Bremner, J. D., Southwick, S. M., Darnell, A., and Charney, D. S. 1996. Chronic PTSD in Vietnam combat veterans: Course of illness and substance abuse. *American Journal Of Psychiatry* 153, no. 3:369–75.

Clemens, N. A., Corradi, R. B., and Wasman, M. 1978. The parish clergy as a mental health resource. *Journal of Religion and Health* 17, no. 4:227–32.

Coffey, S. F., Schumacher, J. A., Brady, K. T., and Cotton, B. D. 2007. Changes in PTSD symptomatology during acute and protracted alcohol and cocaine abstinence. *Drug and Alcohol Dependency* 87, nos. 2-3: 241–48.

Corrington, J. E. 1989. Spirituality and recovery: Relationships between levels of spirituality, contentment, and stress during recovery from alcoholism in AA. *Alcoholism Treatment Quarterly* 6, nos. 3/4: 151–65.

Council on Scientific Affairs. 1996. Alcoholism in the elderly. *Journal of the American Medical Association* 275, no. 10:797–801.

Cunningham-Williams, R. M., Cottler, L. B., Compton, W. M., and Spitznagel, E. L. 1998. Taking chances: Problem gamblers and mental health disorders—Results from the St. Louis Epidemiologic Catchment Area study. *American Journal of Public Health* 88:1093–096.

Dann, B. 2002. *Addiction: Pastoral Response*. Nashville: Abingdon.

Diaz, J. D. 2000. Religion and gambling in Sin-City: A statistical analysis of the relationship between religion and gambling patterns in Las Vegas residents. *Social Science Journal* 37, no. 3:453–58.

Edwards, M. E., and Steinglass, P. 1995. Family therapy treatment outcomes for alcoholism. *Journal of Marital and Family Therapy* 21, no. 4:475–509.

Ellison, C. G., and Nybroten, K .A. 1999. Conservative Protestants and opposition to state-sponsored lotteries: Evidence from the 1997 Texas poll. *Social Science Quarterly* 80, no. 2:356–69.

Figley, C. R. 1989. *Helping the Traumatized Family*. San Francisco: Jossey-Bass.

Finlayson, R. E., Hurt, R. D., Davis, L. J., Jr, and Morse, R. M. 1988. Alcoholism in elderly persons: A study of the psychiatric and psychosocial features of 216 inpatients. *Mayo Clinic Proceedings* 63:761–68.

Fiorentine, R., and Hillhouse, M. P. 2000. Drug treatment and 12-step program participation: The additive effects of integrated recovery activities. *Journal of Substance Abuse Treatment* 18:65–74.

Fleming, J. E., and Offord, D. R. 1990. Epidemiology of childhood depressive disorders: A critical review. *Journal of the American Academy of Child and Adolescent Psychiatry* 29:571–80.

Gallup, G. H., and Bezilla, R. 1992. *The Religious Life of Young Americans*. Princeton, N.J.: The George Gallup International Institute.

Gallup, G. H., and Lindsay, D. M. 1999. *Surveying the Religious Landscape: Trends in U.S. Beliefs*. Harrisburg, Pa.: Morehouse.

Goldsmith, M. F. 1989. Proliferating "self help" groups offer wide range of support, seek physician rapport. *Journal of the American Medical Association* 261:2474–475.

Gorsuch, R. L. 1995. Religious aspects of substance abuse and recovery. *Journal of Social Issues* 51, no. 2:65–83.

Grant, B. F., and Harford, T. C. 1995. Comorbidity between DSM-IV alcohol use disorders and major depression: Results of a national survey. *Drug and Alcohol Dependence* 39:197–206.

Grauf-Grounds, C., and Backton, A. 2007. Patterns of conversations between clergy and their parishioners and referral to other professionals. *Journal of Pastoral Care and Counseling* 61:31–38.

Haggerty, K. P., Wells, E. A., Jenson, J. M., Catalano, R. F., and Hawkins, J. D. 1989. Delinquents and drug abuse: A model program for community reintegration. *Adolescence* 24:439–56.

Harwood, H. 2000. Updating estimates of the economic costs of alcohol abuse in the United States: Estimates, update methods, and data. The National Institute on Alcohol Abuse and Alcoholism, National Institutes of Health, Department of Health and Human Services. NIH Publication No. 98-4327.

Hatchett, B. F., Miller, J. B., Solomon, R. V., and Holmes, K. Y. 2007. The clergy: A valuable resource for church members with alcohol problems. *Journal of Pastoral Care and Counseling* 61:39–45.

Hoffmann, J. P. 2000. Religion and problem gambling in U.S. *Review of Religious Research* 41, no. 4:488–509.

Hoge, C. W., Castro, C. A., Messer, S. C., McGurk, D., Cotting, D. I., and Koffman, R. L. 2004. Combat duty in Iraq and Afghanistan, mental health problems, and barriers to care. *New England Journal of Medicine* 351, no. 1:13–22.

Hohmann, A. A., and Larson, D. B. 1993. Psychiatric factors predicting use of clergy. In E. L. Worthington, Jr., ed., *Psychotherapy and Religious Values*, 71–84. Grand Rapids: Baker.

Huntley, D. K., and Phelps, R. E. 1990. Depression and social contacts of children from one-parent families. *Journal of Community Psychology* 18:66–72.

Ingram, B. L., and Lowe, D. 1989. Counseling activities and referral practices of rabbis. *Journal of Psychology and Judaism* 13:133–48.

Johnson, K., Strader, T., Berbaum, M., Bryant, D., Bucholtz, G., Collins, D., and Noe, T. 1996. Reducing alcohol and other drug use by strengthening community, family and youth resiliency. *Journal of Adolescent Research* 11, no. 1:36–67.

Jones, K. B. 2001. *Rest in the Storm: Self-Care Strategies for Clergy and Other Caregivers.* Valley Forge, Pa.: Judson.

Kessler, R. C., Sonnega, A., Bromet, E., Hughes, M., and Nelson, C. B. 1995. Post-traumatic stress disorder in the National Comorbidity Survey. *Archives of General Psychiatry* 52:1048–060.

Koenig, H. G. 2002. *Purpose and Power in Retirement.* Philadelphia: Templeton Foundation Press.

Koenig, H. G., George, L. K., Meador, K. G., Blazer, D. G., and Ford, S. M. 1994. The relationship between religion and alcoholism in a sample of community-dwelling adults. *Hospital and Community Psychiatry* 45:225–31.

Kulka, R. A., Fairbank, J. A., Jordan, K. B., Weiss, D., and Cranston, A. 1990. *Trauma and the Vietnam War Generations: Report of the Findings from the National Vietnam Veterans Readjustment Study.* New York: Brunner/Mazel.

LaGreca, A. J., Akers, R. L., and Dwyer, J. W. 1988. Life events and alcohol behavior among older adults. *Gerontologist* 28:552–58.

Larson, D. B., Swyers, J. P., and McCullough, M. E. 1998. *Scientific Research on Spirituality and Religion.* Rockville, Md.: National Institute for Healthcare Research.

Liberto, J. G., Oslin, D. W., and Ruskin, P. E. 1992. Alcoholism in older persons: A review of the literature. *Hospital and Community Psychiatry* 43:975–84.

Lowe, D. W. 1986. Counseling activities, and referral practices of ministers. *Journal of Psychology and Christianity* 5:22–29.

Mannon, J. D., and Crawford, R. L. 1996. Clergy confidence to counsel and their willingness to refer to mental health professionals. *Family Therapy* 23, no. 3:213–31.

McNulty, P. A. 2005. Reported stressors and health care needs of active duty Navy personnel during three phases of deployment in support of the war in Iraq. *Military Medicine* 170, no. 6:530–35.

Miller, J. W., Naimi., T. S., Brewer, R. D., and Jones, S. E. 2007. Binge drinking and associated health risk behaviors among high school students. *Pediatrics* 119, no. 1:76–85.

Miller, L., Warner, V., Wickramaratine, P., and Weissman, M. 1997. Religiosity and depression: Ten-year follow-up of depressed mothers and offspring. *The Journal of the American Academy of Child and Adolescent Psychiatry* 36, no. 10:1416–425.

Miller, N. S., and Verinis, J. S. 1995. Treatment outcome for impoverished alcoholics in abstinence based programs. *International Journal of Addictions* 30:753–63.

Miller, W. R., and Jackson, K. A. 1995. *Practical Psychology for Pastors.* Englewood Cliffs, N.J.: Prentice-Hall.

Mirand, A. L., and Welte, J. W. 1996. Alcohol consumption among the elderly in a general population, Erie County, New York. *American Journal of Public Health* 86:978–84.

Moos, R., Schaefer, J., Andrassy, J., and Moos, B. 2001. Outpatient mental health care, self-help groups, and patients' 1-year treatment outcomes. *0 57*:1–15.

National Institute on Alcohol Abuse and Alcoholism. (2005). *NIAAA initiative on underage drinking.* Retrieved September 10, 2007, from http://www.niaaa.nih.gov/AboutNIAAA/NIAAASponsoredPrograms/underage, accessed March 2, 2009.

National Research Council. 1999. *Pathological Gambling: A Critical Review.* Washington, D.C.: National Academy Press.

O'Connor, P. G., and Schottenfeld, R. S. 1998. Patients with alcohol problems. *New England Journal of Medicine* 338:592–602.

Orthner, D. K. 1986. *Pastoral Counseling: Caring and Caregivers in The United Methodist Church.* Nashville: General Board of Higher Education and Ministry of The United Methodist Church.

Pardini, D. A., Plante, T. G., Sherman, A., and Stump, J. E. 2000. Religious faith and spirituality in substance abuse recovery: Determining the mental health benefits. *Journal of Substance Abuse Treatment* 19, no. 4:347–54.

Parrott, L. 1993. *Helping the Struggling Adolescent.* Grand Rapids: Zondervan.

Patterson, D. 2003. *Essential Parish Nurse: ABCs for Congregational Health Ministry.* Cleveland: Pilgrim.

Petry, N. M. 2002. How treatments for pathological gambling can be informed by treatments for substance use disorders. *Experimental and Clinical Psychopharmacology* 10, no. 3:184–92.

Regier, D. A., Farmer, M. E., Rae, D. S., Locke, B. Z., Keith, S. J., and Judd, L. L. 1990. Comorbidity of mental disorders with alcohol and other drug abuse. Results from the Epidemiologic Catchment Area (ECA) Study. *Journal of the American Medical Association* 264:2511–518.

Reynolds, W. M. 1995. Depression. In V. B. Van Hasselt and M. Hersen, eds., *Handbook of Adolescent Psychopathology,* 297–348. New York: Lexington Books.

Ritsher, J. B., McKellar, J. D., Finney, J. W., Otilingam, P. G., and Moos, R. H. 2002. Psychiatric comorbidity, continuing care, and self-help as predictors of substance abuse remission 5 years after intensive treatment. *Journal of Studies on Alcohol* 63:709–15.

Room, R., and Greenfield, T. 1993. Alcoholics Anonymous, other 12-step movements and psychotherapy in the US population, 1990. *Addiction* 88:555–62.

Rowatt, G. W. 1989. *Pastoral Care with Adolescents in Crisis.* Louisville: Westminister John Knox.

Schonfeld, L., and Dupree, L. W. 1995. Treatment approaches for older problem drinkers. *International Journal of Addiction* 30:1819–842.

Schutte, K .K., Brennan, P. L., and Moos, R. H. 1994. Remission of late-life drinking problems: A 4-year follow-up. *Alcohol Clinical and Experimental Research* 18:835–44.

Shaffer, H. J., Hall, M. N., and Vander Bilt, J. 1999. Estimating the prevalence of disordered gambling behavior in the United States and Canada: A research synthesis. *American Journal of Public Health* 89:1369–376.

Stinson, F. S., Dufour, M. C., and Bertolucci, D. 1989. Epidemiologic bulletin no. 20: Alcohol-related morbidity in the aging population. *Alcohol Health & Research World* 13:80–87.

Substance Abuse and Mental Health Services Administration (SAMHSA). 2003. *Overview of findings from the 2002 National Survey on Drug Use and Health.* Rockville, Md.: Office of Applied Studies, NHSDA Series H-21, DHHS Publication No. SMA 03–3774.

Substance Abuse and Mental Health Services Administration (SAMHSA). 2005. *Binge alcohol use among persons aged 12 to 20: 2002 and 2003 update.* The National Household Survey on Drug Abuse Report (August 26, 2005). http://oas.samhsa.gov/2k5/youthBinge/youthBinge.htm, accessed March 2, 2009.

Sylvain, C., Ladouceur, R., and Boisvert, J. 1997. Cognitive and behavioral treatment of pathological gambling: A controlled study. *Journal of Consulting and Clinical Psychology* 65, no. 5:727–32.

Tonigan, J. S. 2007. Spirituality and Alcoholics Anonymous. *Southern Medical Journal* 100, no. 4:437–40.

Turner, W. H. 1995. Bridging the gap: Addressing alcohol and drug addiction from a community health perspective. *American Journal of Public Health* 85, no. 6:870–71.

Weaver, A. J. 1995. Has there been a failure to prepare and support parish-based clergy in their role as front-line community mental health workers? A review. *The Journal of Pastoral Care* 49:129–49.

Weaver, A. J., Preston, J. D., and Jerome, L. W. 1999. *Counseling Troubled Teens and Their Families: A Handbook for Pastors and Youth Workers.* Nashville: Abingdon.

Weaver, A. J., Flannelly, L. T., and Preston, J. D. 2003. *Counseling Survivors of Traumatic Events: A Handbook for Pastors and Other Helping Professionals.* Nashville: Abingdon.

Wechsler, H., Seibring, M., Liu, I., and Ahl, M. 2004. Colleges respond to student binge drinking: Reducing student demand or limiting access. *Journal of American College Health* 52:159–68.

Welte, J. W. 1998. Stress and elderly drinking. In Gomberg, E. S. L., Hegedus, A.M., and Zucker, R. A., *Alcohol Problems and Aging.* NIAAA Research Monograph No. 33. NIH Pub. No. 98-4163. Bethesda, Md.: NIAAA.

Wills, T. A., Yaeger, A. M., and Sandy, J. M. 2003. The buffering effect of religiosity for adolescent substance use. *Psychology of Addictive Behaviors* 17, no. 1:24–31.

Wright, L. S., Frost, C. J., and Wisecarver, S. J. 1993. Church attendance, meaningfulness of religion, and depression symptomatology among adolescents. *Journal of Youth and Adolescence* 22:559–68.

CPSIA information can be obtained at www.ICGtesting.com
Printed in the USA
LVOW011044291112

309241LV00007B/263/P

9 780800 662615